Women Need Good Credit Too

Monthly Planner for Establishing and Maintaining Good Credit

DR. DONNA PRUDHOMME

CREDIT
EDUCATION SCHOOL

Written by Dr. Donna Prudhomme
Illustrated by Charlotte Pabalan

Printed in the United States of America
ISBN 978-1-7331188-2-8

www.crediteducationschool.com
info@crediteducationschool.com

Disclaimer

The author is not a lawyer. For legal advice, please seek an attorney as the contents of this book should not be construed as legal advice in any way. Every effort has been made to ensure the accuracy of the information within this book. However, we cannot be held liable for any omissions, errors, or inconsistencies. You are solely responsible for actions taken (or not taken) based on the information contained in this book.

This planner belongs to

____

Contents

Dedication

This planner is dedicated to my beloved sister, Nasheka Powell, affectionately known as Shay. Your presence is deeply missed every day, but I feel your spirit guiding me on this journey.

I ♡ Love You Sissy

Acknowledgements

First and foremost, I want to thank God for the opportunity to educate and empower girls around the world about the importance of credit.

I am deeply grateful to my loving husband, whose unwavering support has been a cornerstone of all my endeavors. You witnessed my exhaustion and the challenges of failed business ventures, yet you never told me to give up. I remember you saying, "You are always working hard, and eventually, something will happen." Your belief in me has been a constant source of strength and encouragement.

To my son and daughter, every pursuit I've undertaken has been for you, with the hope of making your lives better. Thank you for your patience and encouragement, especially during the times when things didn't go as planned. You have witnessed my struggles, and I am confident that you have learned from my mistakes. Your strength and resilience continue to inspire me, and I know these experiences will make you both even stronger.

Hey Girl, Hey!

I am so excited you've chosen to invest in yourself by picking up this planner, Women Need Good Credit Too. As women, we wear so many hats: we're daughters, sisters, mothers, friends, employees, business owners, caregivers, and everything in between. It often feels like there's no time for anything else– but I promise you, your financial future is worth the time and attention you're about to give it.

Throughout my career, I've had the privilege of working with incredible women who, just like you, are balancing life's demands while trying to manage their finances. I've seen how important it is for women to take control of their financial destinies, but I also know how challenging it can be to focus on something like credit when there are so many other things vying for your attention.

That's why I created this planner–so that you can easily navigate the world of credit without feeling overwhelmed. I've broken it down into practical steps that you can apply at your own pace. Whether you're just starting to build credit, looking to improve your score, or simply trying to maintain the progress you've made, this planner is here to help you along the way.

Credit is more than just a number–it's a tool that can open doors to the life you dream of, whether that's buying a home, starting your own business, or gaining the financial freedom to live life on your own terms. But in order to make it work for you, you need to understand it, manage it, and take action. That's what we're going to do together.

You've already shown a commitment to your future by picking up this planner, and I'm so proud of you for that. No matter where you're starting from, know that you have the power to build the financial future you want. This planner is your guide, and I'm here every step of the way to help you succeed–just like a friend, a mentor, and a cheerleader rolled into one.

So, let's do this! Take your time and breathe through the process. You deserve a strong, secure financial future, and you have everything it takes to make it happen.

Dr. Donna Prudhomme

Dr. Donna Prudhomme
Board Certified Credit Consultant

“Empowered women build strong credit—because when you take control of your financial future, you unlock the power to create the life you deserve.”

Introduction

Congratulations on taking the first step toward mastering your credit! This planner is designed to be your trusted companion on your journey to financial empowerment, offering you practical tools, actionable steps, and unwavering support to help you build and maintain strong credit.

As women, we know how to juggle—whether it's balancing work, family, or personal goals. In the midst of our busy lives, it can be easy to forget to prioritize our own financial well-being. But the truth is, investing in your financial health is one of the most important investments you can make in yourself.

This planner will help you understand the ins and outs of credit—how it works, how to improve your score, and how to make the most of your financial decisions. Each month, you'll have the opportunity to set new goals, track your progress, and discover strategies to stay on top of your credit game.

Inside this planner, you'll find:

- Easy-to-understand credit education that breaks down complex topics into manageable steps.
- Actionable tips to help you take control of your credit and build a strong foundation.
- Motivational support to encourage you along the way and remind you that you are more than capable of achieving your financial goals.

At the heart of this planner is the belief that you deserve financial freedom, peace of mind, and the ability to make decisions that align with your dreams and values.

Remember, this journey is all about progress, not perfection. Small, consistent steps will lead you toward lasting financial freedom. So, let's dive in, get organized, and start building the credit and financial future you deserve!

PART ONE

Understanding Credit and Its Importance

What is Credit?

Credit is a financial tool that allows individuals to borrow money or access goods or services with the agreement to repay the lender over time. Credit can come in the form of loans, credit cards, and other financial products. When you use credit, the lender records the transaction, and that record contributes to your overall financial profile, known as your credit history.

Understanding credit empowers you to make smart financial decisions, open doors to new opportunities, and achieve long-term financial goals.

Why Credit Matters for Women

Credit plays a crucial role in financial independence and stability, both of which are especially important for women. With good credit, you can secure better interest rates on loans, reduce expenses on large purchases, and position yourself for financial resilience. Credit can also influence life decisions, like starting a business, buying a home, or funding education.

For women, in particular, good credit provides a foundation for financial freedom, which can be empowering in relationships, work, and personal endeavors. Whether single, married, or in transition, a strong credit history can be a powerful asset.

Types of Credit:

Revolving, Installment, Open, and Service Credit

1. Revolving Credit

- This type of credit includes credit cards and lines of credit, allowing you to borrow up to a limit and repay based on your monthly usage. The outstanding balance "revolves" month to month. You're only required to make minimum payments, but paying in full can help you avoid interest.
- Example: Credit cards are a common form of revolving credit.

2. Installment Credit

- With installment credit, you borrow a specific amount and agree to repay it in fixed installments over a set period. Most car loans, student loans, and mortgages are examples of installment credit.
- Example: Taking out an auto loan and making monthly payments until the car is paid off.

3. Open Credit

- Open credit refers to accounts where the balance is due in full each month.
- Example: Utility bills are often considered open credit accounts, as they must be paid in full each month.

4. Service Credit

- Is credit extended for services you use and pay for later, such as utilities, internet, or phone services. You receive the service first and pay the bill afterward.
- Example: Your electricity bill, where you use power throughout the month and pay for it afterward. Timely payments help build your credit, while late payments can hurt it.

Credit Score Basics:

FICO, VantageScore, and Other Models

Your credit score is a three-digit number that represents your creditworthiness, or how likely you are to repay borrowed money responsibly. Credit scores range between 300 and 850, with higher scores indicating better credit.

- **FICO Score:** The most widely used scoring model, based on factors like payment history, debt amount, credit age, credit mix, and new credit.

- **VantageScore:** An alternative scoring model with similar factors but slightly different weightings. It's often used by lenders as a complementary tool to the FICO score.

Scores typically fall into these categories:

 **Poor** (300-579)

 **Fair** (580-669)

 **Good** (670-739)

 **Very Good** (740-799)

 **Excellent** (800-850)

The five factors that determine your credit score are:

Payment History (35%) | 192.5 Points
Your track record of paying bills on time, including credit cards, loans, and other debts.

Credit Utilization (30%) | 165 Points
The ratio of your current credit card balances to your credit limits. Lower utilization is better for your score.

Credit History (15%) | 82.5 Points
The length of time your credit accounts have been active. A longer credit history can improve your score.

Credit Mix (10%) | 55 Points
The variety of credit accounts you have, such as credit cards, mortgages, and installment loans.

New Credit (10%) | | 55 Points
The number of recent inquiries and new accounts opened. Opening too many new accounts in a short period can negatively impact your score.

Credit Gem

The sweet spot for credit utilization is 1-10% to enhance your credit score.

Credit Statistics for Women

Women face significant challenges in credit access and management, with several key statistics illustrating these disparities. According to the Consumer Financial Protection Bureau (CFPB), women, on average, have a credit score that is 10 points lower than men. Additionally, a 2022 report from the Federal Reserve found that women are more likely to have a "thin" credit file, meaning they have little or no credit history, which affects their ability to obtain loans or credit cards.

When broken down by race, the disparities are even more pronounced. For example, FICO® data shows that, on average, Black women have a credit score of 596, while white women average a score of 686. Hispanic women typically have a score of 630. This shows that women of color are especially affected by lower credit scores, which can result in higher interest rates, less access to credit, and more financial barriers.

Another notable statistic comes from a 2020 study by Experian, which found that 35% of women had a 'fair" or "poor" credit score (below 650), compared to just 26% of men. However, women are becoming more proactive in improving their credit. According to a survey by Credit Karma, 70% of women reported taking active steps to improve their credit scores, including paying bills on time and managing debt more carefully.

Credit Gem

Paying off debt isn't the only way to boost your credit score. While reducing debt is important, there are other strategies to improve your credit score, such as requesting a credit limit increase. By increasing your available credit without increasing your spending, you lower your credit utilization ratio, which is a major factor in your score.

How Credit Scores Impact Financial Opportunities

Credit scores can significantly impact various aspects of your financial life. A high score can open doors to lower interest rates on loans and credit cards, which means lower costs over time. For example, a woman with an "Excellent" credit score might secure a mortgage with a much lower interest rate than someone with "Fair" credit, resulting in substantial savings over the life of the loan.

Good credit can also:

- Improve approval chances for renting apartments
- Lower insurance premiums in some states
- Increase your chances of approval for business loans or credit lines

Hard and Soft Inquiries

1. Hard Inquiry (or Hard Pull): A hard inquiry occurs when a lender or financial institution checks your credit report as part of a lending decision, such as when you apply for a credit card, mortgage, or car loan.

- **Impact on Credit:** Hard inquiries can slightly lower your credit score for a short period (usually a few points).
- **Example:** Applying for a new credit card or a loan.

2. Soft Inquiry (or Soft Pull): A soft inquiry happens when your credit is checked for purposes other than lending, like a background check, pre-approval offers, or your own personal credit check.

- **Impact on Credit:** Soft inquiries do not affect your credit score.
- **Example:** Checking your own credit score, a company offering you a preapproved credit card, or an employer checking your credit as part of a job application.

Credit Gem

Hard inquiries can impact your credit score, while soft inquiries do not.

Common Credit Myths

Credit often comes with misconceptions that can lead to financial missteps. Here are a few myths debunked:

Myth 1: Checking your credit will hurt your score.

- **Truth:** Only "hard" inquiries–like those made by lenders when you apply for credit–can impact your score. Checking your own credit report is considered a "soft" inquiry and has no effect on your score.

Myth 2: Closing a credit card will improve your score.

- **Truth:** Closing an account can reduce your available credit and increase your credit utilization ratio, which could actually lower your score. It's often better to keep older accounts open.

Myth 3: Paying off debt will immediately remove it from your report.

- **Truth:** While paying off debt is beneficial, it doesn't erase it from your report right away. Positive credit history remains for up to 10 years, while negative items may stay on your report for up to 7 years.

Credit Gem

Your credit score is a reflection of your financial habits, not your wealth. A common misconception is that only wealthy individuals can have good credit scores, but that's not true. Building and maintaining good credit is about consistent, responsible financial behavior, such as paying bills on time, managing credit wisely, and avoiding excessive debt. It's the habits that count, not the amount of money you have.

“Building credit is not just about numbers—it's about claiming your financial independence and creating a foundation for your dreams to flourish.”

PART TWO

Building Strong Credit

Building strong credit takes time, consistency, and smart financial habits. This section will provide you with actionable steps to begin or rebuild your credit journey and set yourself up for financial success.

Starting with No Credit or Rebuilding from Scratch

Whether you're starting fresh or working to rebuild, the good news is that you can take steps to establish or strengthen your credit profile.

- **For New Credit Builders:** If you're new to credit, you can start with simple tools like a secured credit card or a credit-builder loan. These allow you to build positive payment history while keeping spending manageable.

- **For Credit Rebuilders:** Focus on establishing on-time payments and reducing any outstanding debt. By consistently paying bills on time and lowering credit balances, you'll start to see gradual improvements in your credit score.

TIPS	
TIPS	**1.** Start small with one credit account or loan. **2.** Set up automatic payments to ensure you never miss a payment. **3.** Monitor your credit regularly to track your progress and catch any issues early.

Types of Accounts to Open and When

Different types of accounts can help you build a balanced credit profile. Here's a look at options for each stage of credit-building:

1. Secured Credit Card: Ideal for beginners and those with no credit history. You make a deposit that acts as your credit limit, and regular, on-time payments will help build your score.

2. Credit-Builder Loan: Offered by some banks and credit unions, this loan allows you to "borrow" a small amount, which you repay over time. Once repaid, the funds are released to you, along with positive credit history.

3. Retail Credit Card: Many stores offer credit cards with low limits. These can help with building credit, but be cautious of high interest rates and try to pay off the balance each month.

TIPS	**1.** Start with one or two accounts and prioritize paying them on time. **2.** Only open new accounts if you can manage them responsibly.

Establishing a Credit History

Building credit history is a long-term process, and every small step counts. Here are a few tips for establishing a solid credit foundation:

- **Pay On Time:** Payment history makes up about 35% of your credit score, so it's essential to pay every bill on time, even if it's just the minimum payment.
- **Limit Credit Applications:** Each time you apply for credit, it results in a "hard inquiry," which can temporarily lower your score. Apply for new credit only when necessary.

- **Use Credit Responsibly:** Aim to use no more than 30% of your credit limit on each account. For example, if your credit card has a $1,000 limit, try to keep the balance under $300. Remember, the sweet spot is credit utilization between 1-10%.

TIPS	**1.** Set up reminders or automatic payments to ensure on-time payments. **2.** Aim for a positive account history that spans at least 6-12 months before applying for additional credit.

Secured Credit Cards and Loans

Secured credit cards and loans are excellent tools for those new to credit or those rebuilding. Here's how they work:

- **Secured Credit Card:** With a secured card, you make a deposit (often around $200- 500), which acts as your credit limit. Using the card and paying the balance each month helps build positive payment history. Some secured cards even "graduate" to unsecured cards after several months of good use.

- **Credit-Builder Loan:** This is a type of loan where you make monthly payments on a small amount of money held by the lender. After repayment, the money is released to you, and your positive payment history is reported to the credit bureaus.

TIPS	**1.** Look for secured cards or credit-builder loans with no annual fees or low fees. **2.** Use these accounts responsibly, as they're stepping stones to future credit opportunities.

The Importance of Payment History

Payment history is the most critical factor in your credit score, so prioritizing on-time payments is essential. Late payments can harm your score, and missed payments stay on your report for up to 7 years.

Best Practices:

- **Automate Payments:** Set up automatic payments or reminders for all your bills to avoid late payments.
- **Pay More Than the Minimum:** If you can, pay more than the minimum to reduce interest charges and pay off debt faster.
- **Resolve Issues Quickly:** If you miss a payment, catch up as soon as possible to minimize the impact.

Tips for Building Credit Responsibly

Building good credit is a steady journey. Here are some tips to help you along the way:

1. Stay Within Your Means: Avoid the temptation to use credit for unnecessary purchases. Stick to essentials and budget for any expenses.

2. Keep Your Oldest Accounts Open: The length of your credit history impacts your score, so keeping older accounts open can benefit your credit in the long term.

3. Monitor Your Credit Score Regularly: By checking your score often, you can track your progress and address issues early. Many banks and credit card companies offer free credit monitoring tools.

4. Avoid Co-Signing Unless Necessary: Co-signing a loan or credit card for someone else means you're responsible for their debt if they can't pay. This can risk your credit if they miss payments.

- **5. Check Your Credit Report Annually:** Obtain your free credit report from each of the three credit bureaus (Experian, Equifax, and TransUnion) once a year at AnnualCreditReport.com.

“Building credit is a journey, not a destination. Every step you take brings you closer to financial freedom.”

PART THREE

Credit Reports and Credit Monitoring

What is a Credit Report?

A credit report is a detailed record of your credit activity and history. It's used by lenders to assess your creditworthiness when you apply for loans, credit cards, or even jobs. Your credit report contains the following:

- **Personal Information:** Your name, address, Social Security number, and employment history.
- **Credit Accounts:** Details of credit accounts like credit cards, loans, and mortgages. It includes your credit limit or loan amount, payment history, and current balance.
- **Credit Inquiries:** A list of companies or lenders who have recently accessed your credit report. There are two types of inquiries: soft (no impact on your score) and hard (can lower your score slightly).
- **Public Records:** Information like bankruptcies, foreclosures, or liens, which can negatively affect your credit.

TIP	Regularly reviewing your credit report ensures accuracy and helps you stay on top of your financial status.

Who are the Credit Bureaus?

The three major credit bureaus–**Equifax, Experian, and TransUnion**–collect and maintain information on your credit activity. While each bureau collects similar information, they may have slight differences in how they report it. This is why your credit score might vary between bureaus.

Important Contacts:

- Equifax: www.equifax.com
- Experian: www.experian.com
- TransUnion: www.transunion.com

TIP

It's wise to check your credit report from each bureau annually to ensure all information is consistent and accurate.

How to Access Your Credit Report for Free

Under federal law, you're entitled to a free credit report from each credit bureau every 12 months through AnnualCreditReport.com. This website allows you to access your reports securely and check for errors or signs of fraud.

Steps:

1. Go to AnnualCreditReport.com.
2. Fill out the request form with your information.
3. Review each report carefully, checking for any discrepancies or inaccuracies.

Credit Gem

You can stagger your reports throughout the year by checking one bureau every four months to monitor your credit year-round.

How to Read Your Credit Report

Reading a credit report can feel overwhelming at first, but breaking it down into sections helps make sense of it. Here's what to look for in each section:

- **Personal Information:** Check for correct name, address, and employment history. Any unfamiliar information could be a red flag for identity theft.
- **Credit Accounts:** Review each account's balance, credit limit, payment history, and status (open or closed). Ensure all details are accurate.
- **Credit Inquiries:** Look for any unfamiliar hard inquiries, which might indicate fraudulent activity.
- **Public Records:** If you have any bankruptcies, foreclosures, or liens, make sure they're reported accurately.

Credit Gem

Take notes on any items that seem incorrect or unfamiliar, as you'll need this information for any disputes.

The Importance of Credit Monitoring

Credit monitoring helps you stay on top of changes in your credit report and alerts you to potential identity theft. Many financial institutions offer free credit monitoring tools, or you can subscribe to a service for more comprehensive protection.

Benefits of Credit Monitoring

- **Alerts to New Activity:** Immediate alerts if a new account is opened in your name or if there are changes to your credit report.
- **Fraud Protection:** Credit monitoring services can help prevent identity theft by catching unauthorized activities early.
- **Score Tracking:** Many services allow you to track your score over time, which can be helpful as you work toward credit goals.

Popular Credit Monitoring Services

- **Credit Karma:** Free credit monitoring with access to credit reports from TransUnion and Equifax.
- **Experian CreditWorks:** A service from Experian that provides daily score updates, monitoring, and alerts.
- **Equifax Complete:** A paid service offering alerts, fraud support, and identity theft insurance.

How to Dispute Inaccuracies on Your Credit Report

If you find errors on your credit report, disputing them is essential, as inaccuracies can lower your score and affect your financial future. Here's a step-by-step guide to disputing errors:

1. **Gather Documentation:** Collect any documents that support your claim, such as bank statements, receipts, or correspondence with creditors.

2. **Contact the Credit Bureau:** File a dispute with the bureau reporting the error. You can do this online, by phone, or by mail.
   - **Equifax:** Visit their website or call 866-349-5191.
   - **Experian:** File a dispute online or call 888-397-3742.
   - **TransUnion:** Dispute online or call 800-916-8800.

   (Contact information is subject to change.)

3. **File a Dispute:** When filing, explain the error clearly and provide copies of your supporting documents. Credit bureaus typically have 30 days to investigate.

4. **Follow Up:** Check back with the bureau to confirm that the dispute was resolved. If you're unsatisfied with the result, you may need to reach out to the creditor directly or seek additional help.

Credit Gem

Keep a record of all dispute-related correspondence and document any responses from the bureaus.

How Long Do Items Stay on Your Credit Report

Knowing how long information remains on your credit report can give you insight into how certain actions impact your score over time. Here's a breakdown:

- **On-Time Payments:** Positive history stays for up to 10 years.
- **Late Payments:** Negative information remains for 7 years from the date of the missed payment.
- **Collections:** Collection accounts stay for 7 years.
- **Bankruptcies:** Chapter 7 bankruptcy remains for 10 years; Chapter 13 for 7 years.
- **Hard Inquiries:** Remain for 2 years, though their impact on your score diminishes over time.

Credit Gem

If you've resolved old issues, rest assured that time can help your score recover. Practicing good habits consistently is the best way to improve your credit over time.

Tips for Effective Credit Monitoring

Credit monitoring can be easy and cost-effective with the right approach. Here are some tips for effective credit monitoring:

1. Set Alerts: Many services allow you to set alerts for specific changes, like account openings or new inquiries.

2. Check Reports Regularly: Aim to review your report at least once every quarter. This helps you catch any errors or signs of fraud early.

3. Keep an Eye on Old Accounts: Sometimes, dormant accounts can be hacked or experience fraudulent activity, so include these in your monitoring routine.

4. Take Action Quickly: If you receive an alert about suspicious activity, follow up immediately to prevent further damage.

Credit Gem

Monitoring and managing your credit report are foundational steps in maintaining good credit health.

"Your credit is a reflection of your choices. Take control, build wisely, and watch your future transform."

PART FOUR

Managing and Reducing Debt

Managing debt can feel overwhelming at times, but remember, every small step you take brings you closer to financial freedom. Stay focused on your goals, create a realistic plan, and celebrate your progress along the way. With consistency and determination, you have the power to take control and build a brighter financial future!

Understanding Types of Debt

Not all debt is created equal. There are different types of debt, each with its own characteristics and implications. Knowing these types can help you prioritize payments and strategize repayment.

- **Credit Card Debt:** This is a form of revolving debt, often carrying high-interest rates. If left unpaid, it can quickly grow, creating a debt spiral. Credit card debt is usually one of the most expensive forms of debt to carry.

- **Student Loans:** Generally considered "good debt" because it's an investment in your future, student loans usually come with lower interest rates than credit cards. Federal student loans often have more flexible repayment options than private ones.

- **Mortgage Loans:** A mortgage is also viewed as "good debt," as it allows you to build home equity over time. Mortgages typically have lower interest rates and can provide tax benefits.

- **Personal Loans:** Personal loans are usually unsecured and can have varying interest rates. They're sometimes used for consolidating higher-interest debt, like credit cards, but they should be repaid on time to avoid further debt.

- **Auto Loans:** Used to finance vehicles, auto loans are secured by the car itself. The downside is that vehicles depreciate quickly, so it's best to keep these loans manageable to avoid being "upside down" (owing more than the car's value).

Credit Gem

If possible, prioritize paying off high-interest debt first, as it accumulates faster.

Assessing Your Debt-to-Income Ratio

Your **debt-to-income (DTI)** ratio is a critical measure that lenders use to assess your ability to manage monthly payments and repay debts. Calculating your DTI ratio can help you understand how much of your income goes toward paying down debt and guide your decisions for reducing it.

How to Calculate DTI:

1. Add up all your monthly debt payments, including rent/mortgage, credit cards, student loans, auto loans, etc.
2. Divide the total by your gross monthly income.
3. Multiply by 100 to get your DTI percentage.

Example: If your monthly debt payments are **$1,200** and your gross monthly income is **$4,000**, your DTI is (1200 ÷ 4000) × 100 = **30%.**

Recommended DTI Ratios

- **Ideal:** Below 20% for unsecured debt and below 36% for total debt.
- **Manageable:** 36%-49%.
- **High Risk:** 50% and above, indicating that a high portion of your income is going toward debt.

> **Credit Gem**
>
> Reducing your DTI ratio can improve your creditworthiness and free up more income for savings and investments.

Strategies for Paying Down Debt

The best approach to paying down debt depends on your financial situation, the type of debt you have, and your personal preferences. Here are two popular methods:

1. The Snowball Method: With this approach, you pay off your smallest debt first, then move to the next smallest. As you eliminate smaller debts, you gain momentum, building confidence as you go.

- **Steps:**
  - List your debts from smallest to largest.
  - Pay the minimum on all debts except the smallest, which you pay extra toward until it's gone.
  - Move to the next debt on the list and repeat.

2. The Avalanche Method: This method focuses on paying down the debt with the highest interest rate first. Although it can take longer to see progress, you save money in the long run by reducing the total interest you pay.

- **Steps:**
  - List your debts from highest to lowest interest rate.
  - Pay the minimum on all debts except the highest interest one, which you pay extra toward until it's gone.
  - Move to the next highest interest debt and repeat.

Credit Gem

Choose the method that feels most manageable for you, as consistency is key.

Debt Consolidation and Refinancing Options

1. Balance Transfer Credit Card: Some credit cards offer 0% APR for a promotional period, allowing you to transfer higher-interest balances and pay down debt without accumulating interest. Be mindful of any fees and ensure you can pay off the balance within the promotional period.

2. Debt Consolidation Loan: A personal loan used to pay off multiple high-interest debts, leaving you with one monthly payment at a lower rate. Debt consolidation loans can be helpful for managing credit card debt but require good credit to qualify for favorable terms.

3. Home Equity Loan or Line of Credit: If you own a home, you may qualify for a home equity loan or line of credit (HELOC) with lower interest rates. However, these are secured by your home, so they come with higher risk.

4. Student Loan Refinancing: For those with private student loans, refinancing can help lower your interest rate. Federal student loans may lose their benefits if refinanced, so evaluate this option carefully.

Credit Gem

Always research fees and interest rates before consolidating or refinancing, and ensure the new arrangement won't leave you with a longer-term debt burden.

Building a Debt-Reduction Plan

A debt-reduction plan helps you stay organized and motivated as you work toward financial freedom. Here's a step-by-step guide to creating your plan:

1. List All Debts: Write down each debt, including the balance, interest rate, and minimum monthly payment.

2. Choose a Repayment Strategy: Decide between the Snowball or Avalanche method, or consider a consolidation plan if appropriate.

3. Set Monthly Goals: Determine how much extra you can allocate each month toward debt and identify specific milestones, like paying off one account in six months.

4. Automate Payments: Set up automatic payments for minimum balances to avoid missed payments and late fees.

5. Track Your Progress: Regularly update your list and check off debts as they're paid off.

Credit Gem

Consistently working on your plan, even if you're paying small amounts, can have a big impact over time.

Reducing High-Interest Debt

High-interest debt, such as credit card debt, can be challenging to reduce, but some practical steps can help:

1. Negotiate Interest Rates: Contact your credit card issuer to see if they can lower your rate, especially if you have a history of on-time payments.

2. Cut Down Unnecessary Expenses: Review your budget and cut back on discretionary spending. Use these savings to make larger payments toward high-interest debts.

3. Increase Your Income: Consider side jobs or freelance work to boost your income. Allocate extra earnings toward your debt.

4. Use Windfalls Wisely: Apply any tax refunds, bonuses, or unexpected funds directly to your highest-interest debt for faster reduction.

Credit Gem

Every little bit counts. Even $10 extra toward high-interest debt each month can reduce your total balance faster.

Maintaining a Debt-Free Lifestyle

Once you're free of debt or have significantly reduced it, staying debt-free is crucial for longterm financial health. Here are some strategies to avoid falling back into debt:

1. Build an Emergency Fund: Having 3-6 months' worth of expenses saved helps cover unexpected costs, reducing your reliance on credit.

2. Limit Credit Card Use: Only use credit cards for planned expenses and pay the balance in full each month to avoid interest charges.

3. Create a Monthly Budget: A budget helps you allocate funds wisely, ensuring you have enough for expenses, debt repayment, and savings.

4. Track Your Spending: Regularly monitor your bank and credit card statements to ensure you're staying within your budget.

Credit Gem

Practicing responsible credit habits can prevent debt accumulation and support your credit score.

Tackling and managing debt can be challenging, but it's possible with a solid plan and steady progress. Taking control of your debt is a powerful step toward achieving financial freedom.

"A woman with good credit is not just financially savvy; she's paving the way to a future filled with possibilities and freedom."

PART FIVE

Credit Repair and Disputes

Understanding Your Rights: The Fair Credit Reporting Act

The Fair Credit Reporting Act (FCRA) is a law designed to promote accuracy, fairness, and privacy in the collection, use, and reporting of information in credit reports. Under the FCRA:

- **You have the right to dispute any inaccuracies** on your credit report with the credit bureaus.
- **Creditors must report accurate information.** If they report wrong information, you can have it corrected.
- **Negative information must be removed after 7 years** unless it's related to bankruptcy, which can remain for up to 10 years.
- **You can receive a free report** every 12 months from the three major credit bureaus.

Understanding your rights allows you to confidently take action when you see discrepancies on your report. It's your financial history, and you should ensure it's accurate.

Common Reasons for Disputing Items on Your Report

You may find that your credit report contains information that is incorrect, and disputing these items can improve your credit score. Some common reasons for disputing items include:

- **Incorrect account details:** This could include wrong dates, account numbers, or statuses (e.g., "paid" listed as "unpaid").
- **Fraudulent accounts or transactions:** If someone has opened an account in your name or made unauthorized charges, you can dispute these.
- **Inaccurate late payments:** If you have records of on-time payments but the report shows a late payment, you can dispute it.
- **Outdated information:** Some negative items remain on your report beyond the time limit (7 or 10 years).
- **Duplicate entries:** Sometimes the same debt is listed multiple times or reported incorrectly, negatively affecting your score.

By identifying these errors, you're one step closer to a clean, accurate credit report.

Step-by-Step Guide to Disputing Errors

Disputing an error on your credit report doesn't have to be complicated. Here's a simple step-by-step guide:

1. Obtain Your Credit Reports: Get your free credit reports from all three major bureaus.

2. Identify the Errors: Go over each section of your credit report and highlight any inaccuracies.

3. Document the Discrepancy: Gather proof of the error (e.g., bank statements, payment receipts).

4. Write a Dispute Letter: Send a dispute letter to the credit bureau and to the creditor involved, including details of the error and supporting documentation.

5. Wait for the Response: The credit bureau will investigate and typically respond within 30 days.

6. Follow Up: If the error is fixed, verify that all three credit bureaus have updated the report. If not, escalate the issue.

Working with Credit Repair Agencies: What to Know

Credit repair agencies can help you dispute errors, but you should approach this with caution. Some things to know:

- **Legitimacy:** Choose a reputable credit repair company with positive reviews. Ensure they don't promise results they can't deliver.
- **Cost:** Be wary of companies that ask for upfront fees. You can repair your credit on your own, free of charge.
- **What They Do:** A credit repair agency can help you dispute errors, but they cannot create new credit histories for you. They'll assist you in addressing inaccuracies, but ultimately, your financial habits will determine your credit health.
- **Your Rights:** You are entitled to dispute errors yourself at no cost, so be sure you're comfortable with any service fees.

Credit Gem

Disputing errors on your credit report can improve your score. If you find inaccuracies on your credit report, disputing them is not only your right, but it can also lead to a higher credit score. Errors like incorrect late payments or wrong balances can negatively impact your score. Correcting these mistakes can improve your credit standing and ensure you're being judged by accurate information.

Monitoring Progress and Results

It's important to track your credit regularly:

- **Set Up Alerts:** Many credit bureaus offer alerts for changes to your credit report, helping you stay informed of any disputed items.
- **Track Disputes:** Keep a log of the disputes you've made, along with any communication from the credit bureau, to ensure everything is resolved correctly.
- **Check Credit Reports:** After a dispute is resolved, review your credit reports to ensure the changes have been made.

"Invest in your credit like you invest in your dreams—both are worth every bit of effort and care."

PART SIX

Budgeting for Financial Wellness

Creating a Budget with Credit Goals in Mind

Creating a budget that includes credit goals is an essential step in managing your finances. A budget gives you control over your money, helping you stay on track and achieve your financial objectives. To begin:

1. List All Sources of Income: Include your salary, side gigs, freelance work, or any passive income. This will be the base for your budgeting process.

2. Track Your Monthly Expenses: Categorize your expenses into fixed (e.g., rent, utilities, subscriptions) and variable (e.g., food, entertainment, clothing). This helps you see where your money is going.

3. Allocate Funds for Debt Repayment: Make sure your budget prioritizes paying down high-interest debt. By putting extra money toward credit card payments or loans, you'll reduce the total amount paid in interest, ultimately helping you pay off your debt faster.

4. Build Savings: Ensure you allocate money towards savings. Whether it's for emergencies, retirement, or future goals, having savings can reduce the need to rely on credit when unexpected costs arise.

5. Set Credit-Related Goals: These might include paying off a specific credit card, improving your credit score, or lowering the overall balance of your debt. By including these goals in your budget, you'll ensure they're a priority.

- Example: If your goal is to reduce credit card debt by $1,000 in the next 6 months, set aside a specific amount of money each month to work toward that goal.

> **Credit Gem**
>
> By integrating your credit goals into your budgeting plan, you're setting yourself up for a solid financial foundation while also working to improve your credit health.

Balancing Expenses, Debt Repayment, and Savings

A well-balanced budget should allow you to juggle all three: paying off debt, covering your living expenses, and saving for the future. Here's how to find that balance:

1. Debt Repayment Prioritization:

- **High-Interest Debt First:** Focus on paying down high-interest debts (like credit cards) before tackling low-interest debts (like student loans). The reason is simple: high-interest debt costs you more money over time.
- **Use the Debt Snowball or Debt Avalanche Method:** The snowball method involves paying off your smallest debts first to build momentum, while the avalanche method focuses on paying off the debt with the highest interest rate first to save on overall interest.

2. Track Essential vs. Discretionary Spending:

- **Essential Spending:** These are necessary expenses like rent, utilities, groceries, and insurance. Track these carefully to make sure they fit within your budget without excessive overspending.
- **Discretionary Spending:** Things like entertainment, dining out, and shopping fall into this category. It's easy to overspend here, so be mindful of these purchases and find areas where you can cut back.

3. Savings Allocation:

- **Start with an Emergency Fund:** Aim to save at least $500 initially for emergencies, then gradually build up to three to six months' worth of living expenses.
- **Retirement Savings:** Even if it's a small amount, it's important to contribute regularly to retirement accounts like a 401(k) or IRA.
- **Short-Term Savings Goals:** Whether it's saving for a vacation, a new phone, or a home down payment, designate funds for these goals within your budget.

It's important to be realistic with yourself about how much you can save each month while still meeting your debt repayment and living expenses. Adjust your budget as needed and celebrate progress along the way!

Emergency Fund Essentials

An emergency fund is one of the most critical aspects of your financial wellness. Having one in place prevents you from relying on credit when unforeseen circumstances arise, such as medical bills, car repairs, or job loss. Here's how to build and maintain an emergency fund:

1. Start Small and Gradually Increase Savings: If you're just starting, set an initial goal of $500. Once that goal is met, build it to 3-6 months' worth of expenses. The more you save, the more secure you'll feel in case of an emergency.

2. Make It a Priority: An emergency fund is a necessity, not a luxury. Automate transfers into a separate savings account dedicated to emergencies, so you're consistently growing your savings.

3. Don't Touch It (Unless Necessary): Avoid the temptation to dip into your emergency fund unless it's for an actual emergency. Having a clear boundary for this money ensures it's there when you really need it.

By securing your financial safety net, you'll reduce the likelihood of accumulating more debt when life gets unpredictable.

Using Budgeting Apps and Tools

Budgeting apps and tools can make it easier to track your finances and stay organized. Some popular apps that can help you manage your budget and work toward credit-related goals include:

1. Mint: This free app tracks your spending, categorizes your expenses, and even provides free credit score monitoring. Mint helps you set budgets and track your credit card balances, all in one place.

2. YNAB (You Need A Budget): YNAB is a premium budgeting tool that focuses on helping you prioritize your spending, save money, and pay down debt. YNAB's unique approach focuses on giving every dollar a job, helping you plan ahead.

3. EveryDollar: Created by financial expert Dave Ramsey, EveryDollar provides a userfriendly interface to manage your monthly budget. The app's simple design makes it easy to track expenses, set financial goals, and measure progress.

4. Credit Karma: In addition to offering free credit scores, Credit Karma also provides budgeting tools and insights into how credit card balances and other debts are impacting your credit score.

By utilizing these apps, you can ensure that you're consistently tracking your spending, monitoring your credit goals, and adjusting your budget as needed. Research your options and select the app that fits your goal.

Handling Variable Income (for Freelancers, Entrepreneurs, etc.)

If you're a freelancer, entrepreneur, or have a variable income, budgeting becomes more complex. Here's how to manage finances when your income isn't the same each month:

1. **Estimate Your Average Monthly Income:** Review the last 6-12 months of income to get a sense of your average. Use this number as the base for your budget, but always keep in mind that some months might be higher or lower than others.

2. **Budget for Lean Months:** Build flexibility into your budget for months when income is lower. It's better to overestimate expenses during these months than to underestimate them.

3. **Save During High-Earning Months:** When you have a profitable month, allocate extra funds into savings or toward paying off high-interest debt. This will give you a cushion for future lean months.

4. **Separate Personal and Business Finances:** If you're an entrepreneur, keep your personal and business expenses separate. This helps you avoid using business income for personal needs and ensures you're not relying on credit to cover personal expenses.

Credit Gem

Being proactive with your budgeting can provide financial stability, even during unpredictable times.

Setting Financial Milestones and Celebrating Progress

Setting small, achievable financial milestones helps you break down larger goals into manageable steps. This approach not only keeps you on track but also motivates you to continue working toward your financial wellness. Here's how to set and celebrate milestones:

1. **Set Specific Goals:**
   - **Debt-Related Goals:** For example, "I will pay off $500 in credit card debt in the next 3 months."
   - **Savings Goals:** "I will save $1,000 for my emergency fund in the next 6 months."

2. Break Down Long-Term Goals: If your goal is to become debt-free, break it down into smaller milestones, such as paying off a specific credit card or reducing your total debt by a certain percentage.

3. Celebrate Achievements: Celebrating your financial milestones, no matter how small, keeps you motivated. Whether it's treating yourself to a nice meal, taking a break, or simply acknowledging your success, it's important to feel good about your progress.

4. Review and Adjust Regularly: Financial goals should evolve. Periodically review your budget and financial progress, and adjust your goals based on changes in income, expenses, or life circumstances.

Celebrating these milestones reinforces positive financial habits and keeps you focused on achieving even bigger goals in the future.

By implementing these strategies, you'll be well on your way to achieving financial wellness while maintaining healthy credit practices. Budgeting with purpose, staying disciplined with debt repayment, and planning for the future will help you create the financial foundation needed for long-term success.

“Women with strong credit aren’t just building their finances—they’re building their confidence and their future.”

PART SEVEN

Financial Independence and Empowerment

Why Financial Independence Matters for Women

Financial independence is the cornerstone of a woman's empowerment, granting the freedom to make choices based on personal desires rather than financial limitations. It means having control over your money, your career, and your life decisions without relying on others for support.

Why it matters:

- **Empowerment and Autonomy:** With financial independence, you are free to make decisions that align with your values and goals, whether it's pursuing a career you're passionate about, living in your ideal location, or simply living life on your own terms.

- **Security:** Financial independence provides peace of mind, knowing that you can cover your own living expenses and plan for the future. It allows you to weather unexpected events like medical emergencies, job loss, or financial setbacks without relying on others.

- **Break the Cycle of Dependency:** When women are financially independent, they can break free from cycles of debt or dependence on others, building generational wealth and paving the way for future generations.

- **Building Confidence:** Managing your own money and growing your wealth enhances your confidence and self-worth. You begin to trust your ability to make smart financial decisions, which propels you toward even greater success.

Achieving financial independence requires a combination of earning money, saving, budgeting, and investing wisely, all while maintaining strong credit. This foundation allows women to lead their lives without being hindered by financial constraints.

Saving and Investing for the Future

Saving and investing are key components of building wealth and securing financial independence. Saving ensures that you have a financial cushion for emergencies, while investing helps grow your money over time.

1. Why Saving is Essential:

- **Emergency Fund:** First and foremost, save for an emergency fund, which should cover three to six months' worth of living expenses. This gives you a buffer for unexpected expenses and reduces the need to rely on credit when life throws a curveball.

- **Short-Term Goals:** Saving isn't just for emergencies; it's also for things like a vacation, a new car, or a home down payment. Setting up savings accounts dedicated to these goals helps you stay organized and motivated to save.

2. Investing for the Long-Term:

- **Retirement Accounts (IRA, 401(k)):** Contribute regularly to retirement accounts. A 401(k) with employer matching or an IRA can help you build a nest egg over time. Take advantage of tax benefits and compound growth to maximize your savings.

- **Stocks, Bonds, and Mutual Funds:** If you want your money to grow faster than a savings account offers, investing in the stock market is essential. Learn about different types of investments, such as individual stocks, mutual funds, and exchange-traded funds (ETFs). These investments carry risk but also the potential for greater returns over time.

- **Diversification:** Spread your investments across different sectors and asset classes to reduce risk. A diversified portfolio helps minimize losses while still capturing growth.

Start small, but start now. The earlier you begin saving and investing, the more time your money has to grow. Even setting aside a small percentage of your income can yield big results in the future thanks to the power of compound interest.

Protecting Your Credit and Financial Assets in Relationships

While financial independence is important, it's also essential to protect your financial assets and credit, especially when in a relationship, whether it's marriage or cohabitation. Here are ways to safeguard your finances:

1. Keep Finances Separate (If Possible):

- Maintain your own bank accounts and credit cards, especially if you're not yet married. This ensures that your credit and financial history remain yours alone, preventing any surprises or liabilities from your partner's financial issues.

2. Open Communication About Money:

- If you're in a serious relationship, it's crucial to have honest discussions about finances. This includes talking about savings, debts, and how you plan to handle finances together. Clear communication can help prevent misunderstandings and financial stress later on.

3. Credit Scores and Joint Accounts:

- Understand the impact of co-signing loans or opening joint accounts. While this can help build trust, it also means you're responsible for the debt and can be held accountable if payments are missed. Always know where you stand with your joint accounts and communicate about shared financial goals.

4. Legal Protections:

- In the event of separation or divorce, it's important to be aware of your legal rights and protections regarding assets and credit. A prenup or postnup agreement can offer protection in the case of divorce by ensuring both parties' financial rights are respected.

Credit Gem

By protecting your credit and assets in relationships, you maintain your financial autonomy and avoid complications if your relationship changes.

The Role of Insurance and Retirement Accounts

Insurance and retirement accounts are two critical components of financial planning that can help you secure your future and provide protection in case of unexpected events.

1. Insurance as Financial Protection:

- **Health Insurance:** Medical emergencies can be financially devastating without insurance. Make sure you have adequate health coverage to protect yourself and your family from high medical costs.

- **Life Insurance:** If you have dependents, a life insurance policy ensures that your loved ones are financially supported in case something happens to you.

- **Disability Insurance:** If you're unable to work due to illness or injury, disability insurance provides a portion of your income to help cover living expenses.

2. Retirement Accounts for Future Security:

- **401(k) and Employer Matching:** Contribute to your 401(k) if your employer offers matching. This is essentially free money that will grow over time. Always try to contribute enough to get the maximum employer match.

- **Individual Retirement Accounts (IRA):** Whether it's a traditional IRA or a Roth IRA, contributing to an IRA offers tax advantages that can accelerate your retirement savings.

- **Social Security:** Don't forget about Social Security, even though it's not a standalone retirement plan. Stay informed about your benefits and how they contribute to your retirement income.

Credit Gem

Investing in insurance and retirement accounts not only provides peace of mind but also sets you up for financial independence in your later years.

Building Wealth With Real Estate

Real estate is one of the most powerful tools for building lasting wealth, and women are increasingly recognizing its potential to create financial independence and security. Whether through rental properties, house flipping, or commercial investments, real estate offers women unique opportunities to generate passive income, build equity, and capitalize on long-term property appreciation.

- **Generate Passive Income:** Real estate investments, such as rental properties, offer a steady stream of income, allowing women to earn money while building wealth over time.

- **Leverage Financing:** Women can use mortgage financing to purchase properties with a smaller upfront investment and use rental income to cover costs, creating long-term wealth without needing large amounts of capital upfront.

- **Tax Benefits:** Real estate offers tax advantages, such as deductions for mortgage interest and property depreciation, which can significantly enhance financial returns.

- **Diversify Investments:** By investing in various types of properties-residential, commercial, or vacation rentals-women can reduce risk and increase opportunities for income growth.

- **Hedge Against Inflation:** Property values and rents tend to rise over time, making real estate an effective way to protect wealth against inflation and economic downturns.

- **Create a Legacy of Wealth:** With a long-term strategy, real estate can become a powerful tool for building generational wealth and financial independence for women.

Planning for Major Life Goals: Buying a Home, Starting a Business, etc.

Planning for major life goals is a crucial aspect of financial independence. These milestones require careful planning, saving, and possibly securing financing. Here's how to approach common life goals:

1. Buying a Home:

- **Saving for a Down Payment:** Start saving early for a down payment, typically 20% of the home's purchase price. This helps avoid private mortgage insurance (PMI) and can lead to better loan terms.
- **Improve Your Credit:** Your credit score plays a significant role in your mortgage rate. The higher your score, the lower your interest rate and the more affordable your monthly payments will be.
- **Consider Future Expenses:** Homeownership comes with costs beyond the mortgage, such as maintenance, utilities, and property taxes. Plan accordingly to ensure you can afford these ongoing expenses.

2. Starting a Business:

- **Save for Startup Costs:** Research the costs of starting your business and save to cover initial expenses, including marketing, inventory, and legal fees.
- **Build a Business Credit Score:** Like personal credit, your business also has a credit score. Ensure that your business is set up to build and maintain strong credit, which will help you secure loans and favorable terms.
- **Have a Financial Cushion:** Ensure you have enough savings to support both personal and business expenses for at least 3-6 months as your business gets off the ground.

These goals are achievable with careful financial planning, disciplined saving, and proper credit management.

By focusing on financial independence and empowerment, women can gain greater control over their lives, plan for the future with confidence, and create a path to long-term wealth. Whether through saving, investing, or protecting your financial assets, the steps you take today can have a lasting impact on your financial well-being.

Credit Gem

With strategic planning, financing options, and a diversified approach, women can navigate the real estate market and create a strong foundation of wealth.

"When women take charge of their credit, they unlock the door to greater opportunities, security, and empowerment."

PART EIGHT

Credit Goals and Monthly Planning

Setting SMART Credit Goals

Setting SMART goals–Specific, Measurable, Achievable, Relevant, and Time-bound–is a powerful way to take control of your credit journey. Whether you're building credit, repairing it, or maintaining a healthy credit score, setting clear and actionable goals is the first step toward financial success.

S **Specific:** Define your credit goal clearly. Rather than saying "I want to improve my credit score," say "I want to increase my credit score by 50 points in six months by paying off my credit card balances."

M **Measurable:** Make sure you can track your progress. For example, setting a goal to "pay off $500 in credit card debt" is measurable and allows you to track your progress month by month.

A **Achievable:** Your goal should be realistic based on your current financial situation. Don't set yourself up for failure with an unrealistic goal. If paying off $500 a month isn't possible, break it down to a smaller amount.

R **Relevant:** Ensure your goal aligns with your broader financial aspirations. For example, improving your credit score may help you qualify for a mortgage or lower interest rates on loans.

T **Time-bound:** Give yourself a deadline for reaching your goal. It could be a certain date or within a specific time frame, such as three months or six months.

Example SMART goal: "Pay off $200 in credit card debt by the end of the next month to improve my credit score by 30 points."

By creating clear, achievable credit goals, you'll stay motivated and focused on improving your credit health.

Creating Monthly Financial Check-Ins

Setting aside time each month to review your finances ensures you're on track with your credit goals and provides an opportunity to adjust your plan as needed. Monthly financial check-ins are essential for staying accountable and keeping your credit goals in focus.

How to Conduct Your Monthly Check-In:

1. Review Your Credit Report and Score: Check your credit report for any updates, errors, or improvements in your score. Many free tools and apps allow you to monitor your credit score.

2. Assess Your Budget: Review your income and expenses for the month. Are you spending more than planned? Are you allocating enough funds for debt repayment and savings?

3. Track Debt Repayment Progress: Look at how much debt you've paid off and whether you're on track with your repayment plan.

4. Evaluate Savings: Are you contributing to your emergency fund or other savings goals? This is also an important part of your financial health.

5. Celebrate Wins: Acknowledge your progress. Even small victories, like paying off a credit card or saving for an emergency fund, are worth celebrating.

A monthly check-in allows you to adjust your strategy if things aren't going as planned and helps keep your credit goals on track.

Credit Health Checklist for Each Month

A monthly credit health checklist helps you stay organized and focused on maintaining good credit. Here's what you should review every month:

1. Credit Card Balances: Make sure you're staying below 30% of your credit limit. High balances can negatively impact your credit score.

2. Debt Payments: Ensure you're making all your minimum payments on time. Late payments can harm your credit score and incur additional fees.

3. Credit Utilization Ratio: Track your credit utilization. Lower utilization (under 30%) is better for your score. (1-10% is the sweet spot)

4. Credit Inquiries: Check for any hard inquiries on your report. Multiple inquiries in a short period can lower your score.

5. Errors on Your Credit Report: Look for any mistakes or discrepancies that could be affecting your credit. Dispute them as soon as possible.

6. Monitor New Accounts: Keep track of any new credit accounts opened in your name and ensure they are accurate.

By following this checklist each month, you'll be proactive in managing your credit health and prevent surprises.

Reviewing and Adjusting Credit Goals Regularly

Regularly reviewing and adjusting your credit goals ensures they remain aligned with your financial situation and long-term objectives. Life changes, unexpected expenses, or achieving milestones earlier than expected may require you to adjust your goals.

How to Review and Adjust:

1. Evaluate Progress Toward Your Goals: Are you on track to meet your SMART credit goals? If you're ahead, you may want to set more ambitious targets. If you're behind, consider adjusting the timeline or reducing the goal to something more manageable.

2. Reassess Your Financial Situation: Has your income or expenses changed? Are you able to contribute more to debt repayment or savings? Make sure your goals reflect these changes.

3. Be Flexible: Sometimes, external factors (such as medical expenses or an unexpected job loss) may require you to adjust your credit goals. Being flexible will help you stay focused without feeling discouraged.

Adjusting your goals doesn't mean giving up; it's an opportunity to realign your efforts and stay on track with your financial objectives.

Tracking Monthly Expenses, Debt, and Savings Progress

Tracking your monthly expenses, debt, and savings is critical to maintaining control over your financial situation. Here's how you can track your progress effectively:

1. Use Budgeting Apps or Spreadsheets: Tools like Mint, YNAB, or a simple spreadsheet can help you track your expenses and categorize them.

2. Set Realistic Spending Limits: Establish a budget and stick to it, making sure you prioritize debt repayment and savings.

3. Review Debt Payments: Check how much you've paid toward your debts and see if you've reduced balances. Ensure you're paying off high-interest debt first.

4. Monitor Your Savings Goals: Are you contributing to your emergency fund or retirement savings? Small contributions add up over time.

By actively tracking your expenses, debt, and savings, you'll be able to see your financial progress and adjust your plans as needed.

End-of-Month Reflection: Celebrating Wins and Planning for Next Steps

At the end of each month, take time to reflect on your progress and celebrate your wins, no matter how small. Reflection allows you to assess what went well, what didn't, and what you can improve on in the next month.

Reflection Steps:

1. Celebrate Your Wins: Did you pay off a credit card? Did you save more than you planned? Celebrate these accomplishments.

2. Identify Areas for Improvement: What areas of your budget need tweaking? Did you miss any payments? Identify where you can improve in the upcoming month.

3. Set New Goals: Based on your progress, set new, realistic goals for the following month. Use the SMART framework to ensure they are achievable.

4. Prepare for the Next Month: Review your upcoming expenses and adjust your budget or goals as necessary.

Reflection keeps you motivated and focused on your long-term credit goals while ensuring that you're always making progress toward financial wellness.

> "Credit is more than just a number—it's the power to create the life you've always envisioned."

PART NINE

Navigating Life Changes and Credit

Building Credit After Divorce or Separation

Divorce or separation can significantly impact your credit and financial situation. Here's how to rebuild your credit after such a life event:

1. Separate Your Finances: Ensure that all joint accounts are closed or transferred to individual responsibility. Open new accounts in your name only.

2. Check Your Credit Report: Review your credit report to ensure no debts from the marriage are still being reported in your name. Dispute any inaccuracies.

3. Pay on Time: Make sure you pay any remaining bills or debts on time to avoid further damage to your credit score.

4. Consider a Secured Credit Card: If your credit has taken a hit, a secured credit card can help you rebuild it by making on-time payments.

Rebuilding credit after a divorce or separation takes time, but by staying proactive and consistent with your payments, you can gradually improve your financial situation.

Managing Credit During Major Life Events (e.g., New Job, Relocation)

Major life events like starting a new job, moving to a new city, or making a big life transition can affect your credit and finances.

1. Update Your Address and Contact Information: Ensure that your credit bureaus have your updated information to avoid missing important credit notifications.

2. Review Your Budget: Major life changes often bring changes in income, housing costs, and other expenses. Adjust your budget accordingly to reflect these changes.

3. Maintain Credit Payments: Regardless of your new circumstances, keep making timely credit payments to avoid negatively impacting your credit score.

Planning ahead and managing your credit during major life events will ensure that these transitions don't affect your credit negatively.

Credit Tips for New Parents

Being a new parent can bring a lot of joy, but also new financial responsibilities. Here's how to manage credit during this exciting time:

1. Plan for Baby-Related Expenses: Babies come with significant costs. Make sure you budget for baby supplies, healthcare, and any other expenses.

2. Set Up an Emergency Fund: Babies bring unexpected costs. Having an emergency fund can help prevent you from using credit for unforeseen expenses.

3. Review Your Insurance: Make sure your health insurance covers your new baby and that you have enough life insurance to protect your family.

By managing your credit responsibly and planning for the new financial realities of parenthood, you can reduce financial stress during this exciting time.

Dealing with Job Loss or Reduced Income

Job loss or reduced income can cause financial strain, but with the right approach, you can minimize the impact on your credit:

1. Prioritize Essential Expenses: Focus on paying for housing, utilities, food, and any debts that might have a higher interest rate.

2. Communicate with Creditors: If you're unable to make your payments, contact your creditors to discuss deferment options or reduced payment plans.

3. Cut Back on Discretionary Spending: Temporarily reduce your spending on nonessentials to ensure you can cover your necessary expenses.

By managing your expenses carefully and seeking assistance from creditors, you can minimize the impact on your credit while you recover from job loss or reduced income.

Tips for Handling Unexpected Medical Expenses

Unexpected medical expenses can throw off your financial plan and impact your credit if you fall behind on payments. Here's how to handle it:

1. Negotiate with Healthcare Providers: Many medical providers will work with you on payment plans or offer discounts if you pay upfront.

2. Look into Medical Credit Cards: Some medical providers offer credit cards with low or no interest for medical expenses. Just be sure to read the terms carefully.

3. Review Your Health Insurance: Make sure your insurance covers as much of your medical expenses as possible, and appeal any denied claims.

Taking control of your medical bills and exploring all payment options can help prevent them from negatively affecting your credit.

Rebuilding Credit Post-Bankruptcy

If you've filed for bankruptcy, it can take years to fully recover, but you can begin rebuilding your credit right away:

1. Get a Secured Credit Card: A secured card allows you to rebuild credit by making on-time payments while limiting your borrowing capacity.

2. Monitor Your Credit Report: Check your credit report regularly to ensure that any discharged debt is correctly reflected and that no new mistakes have occurred.

3. Create a Budget: After bankruptcy, it's important to live within your means. Use a budget to ensure you don't repeat past financial mistakes.

Rebuilding your credit post-bankruptcy takes time and effort, but with a disciplined approach, you can gradually improve your financial health and regain access to more favorable credit options.

“Good credit is the key that opens doors to a brighter, more independent future. Take the first step today.”

PART TEN

Understanding and Monitoring Your Monthly Financial Activities

- Annual Credit Review
- 52 Week Saving Goals Challenge
- Credit Score Goals
- Credit Score Wheel
- Credit Score Tracker
- Credit Score Chart
- Loan Management
- Monthly Credit Review

Annual Credit Review

52-Week Savings Goal *Challenge*

Goal Amount

Week	Deposit	Balance	Done
1			☐
2			☐
3			☐
4			☐
5			☐
6			☐
7			☐
8			☐
9			☐
10			☐
11			☐
12			☐
13			☐
14			☐
15			☐
16			☐
17			☐
18			☐
19			☐
20			☐
21			☐
22			☐
23			☐
24			☐
25			☐
26			☐

Week	Deposit	Balance	Done
27			☐
28			☐
29			☐
30			☐
31			☐
32			☐
33			☐
34			☐
35			☐
36			☐
37			☐
38			☐
39			☐
40			☐
41			☐
42			☐
43			☐
44			☐
45			☐
46			☐
47			☐
48			☐
49			☐
50			☐
51			☐
52			☐

Credit Score *Goals*

YEAR: GOAL:

MY MONEY MANTRA OF THE YEAR

"

PRIORITIES

1	2	3

ACTION STEPS	ACTION STEPS	ACTION STEPS
1	1	1
2	2	2
3	3	3
4	4	4
5	5	5

NOTES

Credit Score *Wheel*

Monitor your credit score with this colorful monthly wheel tracker, transforming it into an enjoyable activity that helps you track progress and leads you on the path to financial success!

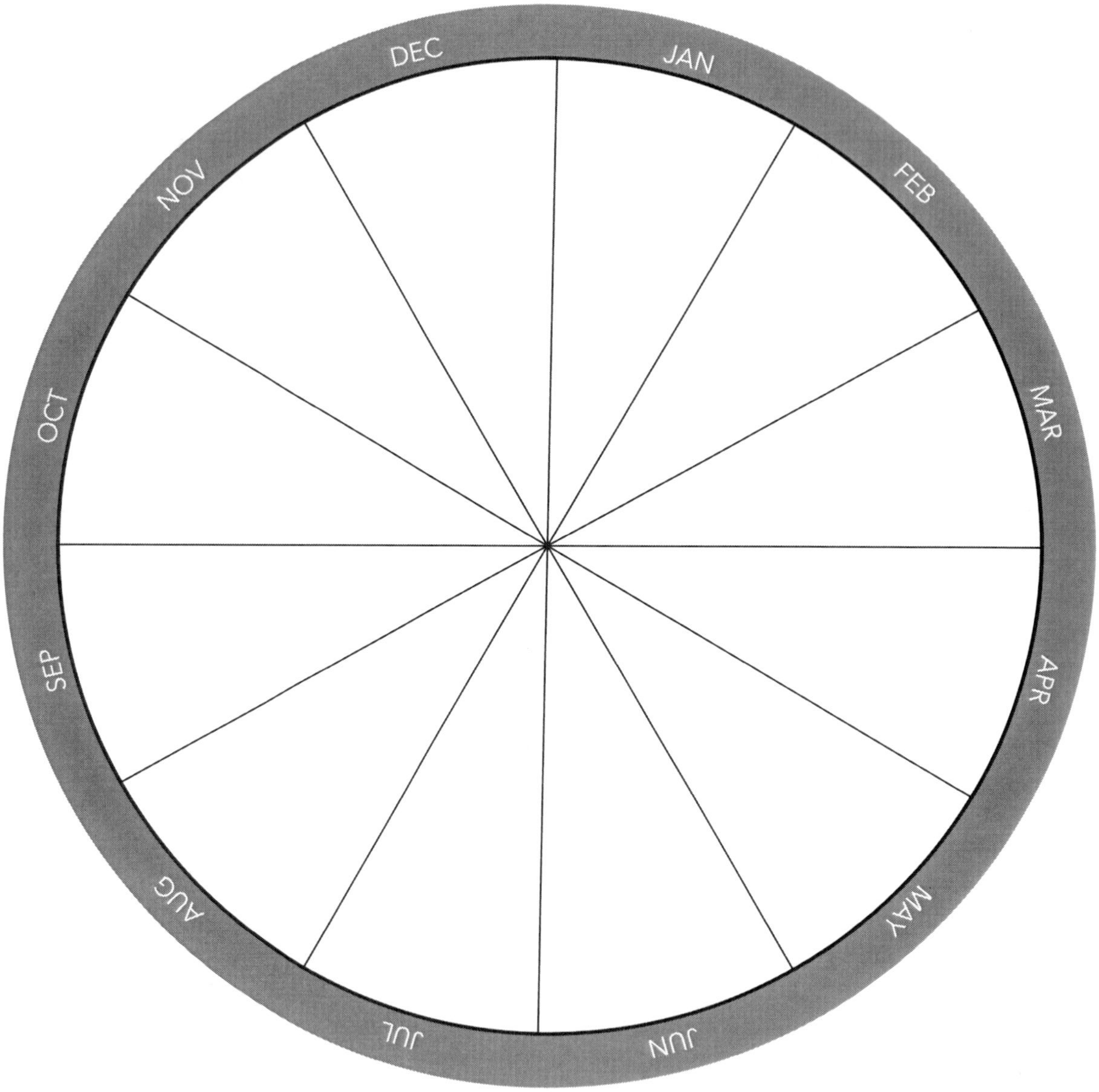

Credit Score Range	Colors
800-850 | Excellent	Dark Green
740-799 | Very Good	Light Green
670-739 | Good	Yellow
580-669 | Fair	Orange
300-579 | Poor	Red

Credit Score *Tracker*

YEAR: CURRENT SCORE: GOAL:

900
850
800
750
700
650
600
550
500
450
400
350
300

JAN FEB MAR APR MAY JUN JUL AUG SEP OCT NOV DEC

Q1

JAN

FEB

MAR

Q2

APR

MAY

JUN

Q3

JUL

AUG

SEP

Q4

OCT

NOV

DEC

Credit Score *Chart*

YEAR:

JANUARY	
TRANSUNION	
EQUIFAX	
EXPERIAN	

FEBRUARY	
TRANSUNION	
EQUIFAX	
EXPERIAN	

MARCH	
TRANSUNION	
EQUIFAX	
EXPERIAN	

APRIL	
TRANSUNION	
EQUIFAX	
EXPERIAN	

MAY	
TRANSUNION	
EQUIFAX	
EXPERIAN	

JUNE	
TRANSUNION	
EQUIFAX	
EXPERIAN	

JULY	
TRANSUNION	
EQUIFAX	
EXPERIAN	

AUGUST	
TRANSUNION	
EQUIFAX	
EXPERIAN	

SEPTEMBER	
TRANSUNION	
EQUIFAX	
EXPERIAN	

OCTOBER	
TRANSUNION	
EQUIFAX	
EXPERIAN	

NOVEMBER	
TRANSUNION	
EQUIFAX	
EXPERIAN	

DECEMBER	
TRANSUNION	
EQUIFAX	
EXPERIAN	

Loan *Management*

LOAN INFORMATION

LOAN NAME	LENDER/ SERVICER	LOAN TYPE	PRINCIPAL AMOUNT	INTEREST RATE	REPAYMENT TERM	MONTHLY PAYMENT	DUE DATE	STATUS
1.								
2.								
3.								

Loan Summary

- **Total Principal Amount:** ______________________________
- **Total Interest:** ______________________________
- **Total Monthly Payment:** ______________________________
- **Total Amount Paid to Date:** ______________________________
- **Remaining Balance:** ______________________________

Repayment Plan

- **Selected Repayment Plan:**
  (Standard, Graduated, Income-Driven, etc.) ______________________________
- **Projected Payoff Date:** ______________________________
- **Interest Savings:**
  (If using a repayment strategy like paying extra) ______________________________

PAYMENT TRACKER

	PAYMENT DATE	PAYMENT AMOUNT	LOAN NAME	PAYMENT METHOD	BALANCE AFTER PAYMENT
JAN					
FEB					
MAR					
APR					
MAY					
JUN					
JUL					
AUG					
SEP					
OCT					
NOV					
DEC					

Payment Reminders

- **Next Payment Due Date:** ________________ • **Reminder Date:** ________________
- **Automatic Payments Setup:** ☐ Yes ☐ No

Forgiveness & Assistance Programs

- **Eligibility for Loan Forgiveness:**
  (e.g., Public Service Loan Forgiveness) ________________________________
- **Application Status:** ________________________________
- **Next Steps:**

____

____

____

MONTHLY NOTES AND ACTION ITEMS

	NOTES	ACTION ITEMS
JAN		
FEB		
MAR		
APR		
MAY		
JUN		
JUL		
AUG		
SEP		
OCT		
NOV		
DEC		

Monthly Credit Review

January

SMART Financial Goals *Worksheet*

JAN	FEB	MAR	APR	MAY	JUN	JUL	AUG	SEP	OCT	NOV	DEC
○	○	○	○	○	○	○	○	○	○	○	○

Description of Goals					
SPECIFIC Cost					
MEASURABLE Monthly Amount					
ATTAINABLE Method/Steps					
REALISTIC Goal Length					
TIMEBOUND Your Timeline					

Notes

Monthly Budget *Planner*

JAN ○ FEB ○ MAR ○ APR ○ MAY ○ JUN ○ JUL ○ AUG ○ SEP ○ OCT ○ NOV ○ DEC ○

INCOME	AMOUNT
TOTAL	

EXPENSES	AMOUNT
TOTAL	

BILLS	AMOUNT
TOTAL	

DEBT	AMOUNT
TOTAL	

SAVINGS	AMOUNT
TOTAL	

SUMMARY	AMOUNT
INCOME	
BILLS	
SAVINGS	
EXPENSES	
DEBT	
TOTAL	

Bills Payment *Calendar*

JAN ○ FEB ○ MAR ○ APR ○ MAY ○ JUN ○ JUL ○ AUG ○ SEP ○ OCT ○ NOV ○ DEC ○

SUN	MON	TUE	WED	THU	FRI	SAT
○ ○	○ ○	○ ○	○ ○	○ ○	○ ○	○ ○
○ ○	○ ○	○ ○	○ ○	○ ○	○ ○	○ ○
○ ○	○ ○	○ ○	○ ○	○ ○	○ ○	○ ○
○ ○	○ ○	○ ○	○ ○	○ ○	○ ○	○ ○
○ ○	○ ○	○ ○	○ ○	○ ○	○ ○	○ ○

Debt Repayment *Plan*

JAN ○ FEB ○ MAR ○ APR ○ MAY ○ JUN ○ JUL ○ AUG ○ SEP ○ OCT ○ NOV ○ DEC ○

Creditor:	Debt Type:
Starting Balance:	Credit Limit:
Repayment Frequency:	Interest Rate:
Goal Pay Off Date:	Min Repayment:

DATE	REPAYMENT	BALANCE	NOTES

Expense *Tracker*

JAN ○ FEB ○ MAR ○ APR ○ MAY ○ JUN ○ JUL ○ AUG ○ SEP ○ OCT ○ NOV ○ DEC ○

DATE	DESCRIPTION	AMOUNT	NOTES

TOTAL ______________________

Credit Card Tracker

JAN ○ FEB ○ MAR ○ APR ○ MAY ○ JUN ○ JUL ○ AUG ○ SEP ○ OCT ○ NOV ○ DEC ○

DATE	CREDIT CARD	CREDIT LIMIT	%RATE	AMOUNT DUE	AMOUNT PAID	BALANCE

Monthly Financial *Reflection*

JAN ○ FEB ○ MAR ○ APR ○ MAY ○ JUN ○ JUL ○ AUG ○ SEP ○ OCT ○ NOV ○ DEC ○

TOTAL INCOME	TOTAL EXPENSES	DIFFERENCE	BALANCE

Biggest Wins this Month

What am I grateful for?

What do I need to improve for next month?

What did I learn by tracking my finances this month?

Wish *List*

JAN	FEB	MAR	APR	MAY	JUN	JUL	AUG	SEP	OCT	NOV	DEC
○	○	○	○	○	○	○	○	○	○	○	○

WISH LIST	HOPE TO PAY	WHERE TO BUY	BOUGHT	SPENT	SAVED	NOTES
			☐			
			☐			
			☐			
			☐			
			☐			
			☐			
			☐			
			☐			
			☐			
			☐			
			☐			
			☐			
			☐			
			☐			
			☐			
			☐			
			☐			
			☐			
			☐			
			☐			
			☐			
			☐			
			☐			
			☐			

Emergency Fund *Tracker*

JAN	FEB	MAR	APR	MAY	JUN	JUL	AUG	SEP	OCT	NOV	DEC
○	○	○	○	○	○	○	○	○	○	○	○

AMOUNT NEEDED:	TARGET DATE:
MONTHLY SAVINGS TARGET:	ACCOUNT:

Progress Tracker

10%	20%	30%	40%	50%	60%	70%	80%	90%	100%

DATE	DEPOSIT	WITHDRAW	NOTES	BALANCE

Notes

Credit Networking and *Mentorship*

JAN ○ FEB ○ MAR ○ APR ○ MAY ○ JUN ○ JUL ○ AUG ○ SEP ○ OCT ○ NOV ○ DEC ○

Networking Goals

What specific goals do you have for networking this month?

1 ____

2 ____

3 ____

Mentorship Goals

What do you want to achieve with the help of a mentor this month?

1 ____

2 ____

3 ____

Identify Networking Opportunities

Events & Workshops

List credit-related events, workshops, or webinars to attend this month:

1 ____

2 ____

3 ____

Online Communities

Identify online groups or forums where you can engage with others focused on credit improvement:

1 ____

2 ____

3 ____

Track Your Progress

Networking Activities

Record your networking activities for the month (e.g., events attended, new connections made):

1 ____

2 ____

3 ____

Mentorship Activities:

Record your interactions with mentors (e.g., meetings, advice received):

1 ____

2 ____

3 ____

Notes

Charity and *Giving*

JAN ○ FEB ○ MAR ○ APR ○ MAY ○ JUN ○ JUL ○ AUG ○ SEP ○ OCT ○ NOV ○ DEC ○

DONATION	ORGANIZATION	DATE GIVEN	VALUE	TAX DEDUCTIBLE

Self-care and Financial *Health*

JAN ○ FEB ○ MAR ○ APR ○ MAY ○ JUN ○ JUL ○ AUG ○ SEP ○ OCT ○ NOV ○ DEC ○

Self-Care Reflection

- **Physical Well-being**

  What physical health activities will you focus on this month?

  o ______________________________

  o ______________________________

- **Emotional & Mental Wellness**

  What mental health activities will you focus on this month?

  o ______________________________

  o ______________________________

- **Time for Self-Care**

  How will you make time for yourself?

  o ______________________________

  o ______________________________

Financial Health Reflection

- **Current Financial Practices**

  What financial habits do you want to maintain or improve this month?

  o ______________________________

  o ______________________________

- **Financial Goals**

  List your financial goals for this month

  - ____
  - ____

- **Financial Self-Care**

  How will you manage financial stress?

  - ____
  - ____

Accountability & Progress

- **Support System**

  Who will help you stay accountable this month?

  - ____
  - ____

- **Tracking Progress**

  How will you monitor your progress? (e.g., weekly check-ins, journaling)

  - ____
  - ____

- **End-of-Month Review Date**

  Set a date to review your goals and make any necessary adjustments

  - ____

February

SMART Financial Goals *Worksheet*

JAN ○ FEB ○ MAR ○ APR ○ MAY ○ JUN ○ JUL ○ AUG ○ SEP ○ OCT ○ NOV ○ DEC ○

Description of Goals					
SPECIFIC Cost					
MEASURABLE Monthly Amount					
ATTAINABLE Method/Steps					
REALISTIC Goal Length					
TIMEBOUND Your Timeline					

Notes

Monthly Budget *Planner*

JAN ○ FEB ○ MAR ○ APR ○ MAY ○ JUN ○ JUL ○ AUG ○ SEP ○ OCT ○ NOV ○ DEC ○

INCOME	AMOUNT
TOTAL	

EXPENSES	AMOUNT
TOTAL	

BILLS	AMOUNT
TOTAL	

DEBT	AMOUNT
TOTAL	

SAVINGS	AMOUNT
TOTAL	

SUMMARY	AMOUNT
INCOME	
BILLS	
SAVINGS	
EXPENSES	
DEBT	
TOTAL	

Bills Payment *Calendar*

JAN ○ FEB ○ MAR ○ APR ○ MAY ○ JUN ○ JUL ○ AUG ○ SEP ○ OCT ○ NOV ○ DEC ○

SUN	MON	TUE	WED	THU	FRI	SAT
○ ○	○ ○	○ ○	○ ○	○ ○	○ ○	○ ○
○ ○	○ ○	○ ○	○ ○	○ ○	○ ○	○ ○
○ ○	○ ○	○ ○	○ ○	○ ○	○ ○	○ ○
○ ○	○ ○	○ ○	○ ○	○ ○	○ ○	○ ○
○ ○	○ ○	○ ○	○ ○	○ ○	○ ○	○ ○

Debt Repayment *Plan*

JAN ○ FEB ○ MAR ○ APR ○ MAY ○ JUN ○ JUL ○ AUG ○ SEP ○ OCT ○ NOV ○ DEC ○

Creditor:	Debt Type:
Starting Balance:	Credit Limit:
Repayment Frequency:	Interest Rate:
Goal Pay Off Date:	Min Repayment:

DATE	REPAYMENT	BALANCE	NOTES

Expense *Tracker*

JAN ○ FEB ○ MAR ○ APR ○ MAY ○ JUN ○ JUL ○ AUG ○ SEP ○ OCT ○ NOV ○ DEC ○

DATE	DESCRIPTION	AMOUNT	NOTES

TOTAL ____________________

Credit Card *Tracker*

JAN	FEB	MAR	APR	MAY	JUN	JUL	AUG	SEP	OCT	NOV	DEC
○	○	○	○	○	○	○	○	○	○	○	○

DATE	CREDIT CARD	CREDIT LIMIT	%RATE	AMOUNT DUE	AMOUNT PAID	BALANCE

Monthly Financial *Reflection*

JAN ○ FEB ○ MAR ○ APR ○ MAY ○ JUN ○ JUL ○ AUG ○ SEP ○ OCT ○ NOV ○ DEC ○

TOTAL INCOME	TOTAL EXPENSES	DIFFERENCE	BALANCE

Biggest Wins this Month

What am I grateful for?

What do I need to improve for next month?

What did I learn by tracking my finances this month?

Wish *List*

JAN	FEB	MAR	APR	MAY	JUN	JUL	AUG	SEP	OCT	NOV	DEC
○	○	○	○	○	○	○	○	○	○	○	○

WISH LIST	HOPE TO PAY	WHERE TO BUY	BOUGHT	SPENT	SAVED	NOTES
			☐			
			☐			
			☐			
			☐			
			☐			
			☐			
			☐			
			☐			
			☐			
			☐			
			☐			
			☐			
			☐			
			☐			
			☐			
			☐			
			☐			
			☐			
			☐			
			☐			
			☐			
			☐			
			☐			
			☐			

Emergency Fund *Tracker*

JAN ○ FEB ○ MAR ○ APR ○ MAY ○ JUN ○ JUL ○ AUG ○ SEP ○ OCT ○ NOV ○ DEC ○

AMOUNT NEEDED:	TARGET DATE:
MONTHLY SAVINGS TARGET:	ACCOUNT:

Progress Tracker

10%	20%	30%	40%	50%	60%	70%	80%	90%	100%

DATE	DEPOSIT	WITHDRAW	NOTES	BALANCE

Notes

Credit Networking and *Mentorship*

JAN ○ FEB ○ MAR ○ APR ○ MAY ○ JUN ○ JUL ○ AUG ○ SEP ○ OCT ○ NOV ○ DEC ○

Networking Goals

What specific goals do you have for networking this month?

1 ____

2 ____

3 ____

Mentorship Goals

What do you want to achieve with the help of a mentor this month?

1 ____

2 ____

3 ____

Identify Networking Opportunities

Events & Workshops

List credit-related events, workshops, or webinars to attend this month:

1 ____

2 ____

3 ____

Online Communities

Identify online groups or forums where you can engage with others focused on credit improvement:

1 ______________________________

2 ______________________________

3 ______________________________

Track Your Progress

Networking Activities

Record your networking activities for the month (e.g., events attended, new connections made):

1 ______________________________

2 ______________________________

3 ______________________________

Mentorship Activities:

Record your interactions with mentors (e.g., meetings, advice received):

1 ______________________________

2 ______________________________

3 ______________________________

Notes

____

____

____

Charity and *Giving*

JAN ○ FEB ○ MAR ○ APR ○ MAY ○ JUN ○ JUL ○ AUG ○ SEP ○ OCT ○ NOV ○ DEC ○

DONATION	ORGANIZATION	DATE GIVEN	VALUE	TAX DEDUCTIBLE

Self-care and Financial *Health*

JAN ○ FEB ○ MAR ○ APR ○ MAY ○ JUN ○ JUL ○ AUG ○ SEP ○ OCT ○ NOV ○ DEC ○

Self-Care Reflection

- **Physical Well-being**

  What physical health activities will you focus on this month?

  ○ ________________________________

  ○ ________________________________

- **Emotional & Mental Wellness**

  What mental health activities will you focus on this month?

  ○ ________________________________

  ○ ________________________________

- **Time for Self-Care**

  How will you make time for yourself?

  ○ ________________________________

  ○ ________________________________

Financial Health Reflection

- **Current Financial Practices**

  What financial habits do you want to maintain or improve this month?

  ○ ________________________________

  ○ ________________________________

- **Financial Goals**

  List your financial goals for this month

  - ______________________________
  - ______________________________

- **Financial Self-Care**

  How will you manage financial stress?

  - ______________________________
  - ______________________________

Accountability & Progress

- **Support System**

  Who will help you stay accountable this month?

  - ______________________________
  - ______________________________

- **Tracking Progress**

  How will you monitor your progress? (e.g., weekly check-ins, journaling)

  - ______________________________
  - ______________________________

- **End-of-Month Review Date**

  Set a date to review your goals and make any necessary adjustments

  - ______________________________

March

SMART Financial Goals *Worksheet*

JAN ○ FEB ○ MAR ○ APR ○ MAY ○ JUN ○ JUL ○ AUG ○ SEP ○ OCT ○ NOV ○ DEC ○

Description of Goals					
SPECIFIC Cost					
MEASURABLE Monthly Amount					
ATTAINABLE Method/Steps					
REALISTIC Goal Length					
TIMEBOUND Your Timeline					

Notes

Monthly Budget *Planner*

JAN ○ FEB ○ MAR ○ APR ○ MAY ○ JUN ○ JUL ○ AUG ○ SEP ○ OCT ○ NOV ○ DEC ○

INCOME	AMOUNT
TOTAL	

BILLS	AMOUNT
TOTAL	

SAVINGS	AMOUNT
TOTAL	

EXPENSES	AMOUNT
TOTAL	

DEBT	AMOUNT
TOTAL	

SUMMARY	AMOUNT
INCOME	
BILLS	
SAVINGS	
EXPENSES	
DEBT	
TOTAL	

Bills Payment *Calendar*

JAN ○ FEB ○ MAR ○ APR ○ MAY ○ JUN ○ JUL ○ AUG ○ SEP ○ OCT ○ NOV ○ DEC ○

SUN	MON	TUE	WED	THU	FRI	SAT
○ ○	○ ○	○ ○	○ ○	○ ○	○ ○	○ ○
○ ○	○ ○	○ ○	○ ○	○ ○	○ ○	○ ○
○ ○	○ ○	○ ○	○ ○	○ ○	○ ○	○ ○
○ ○	○ ○	○ ○	○ ○	○ ○	○ ○	○ ○
○ ○	○ ○	○ ○	○ ○	○ ○	○ ○	○ ○

Debt Repayment *Plan*

JAN ○ FEB ○ MAR ○ APR ○ MAY ○ JUN ○ JUL ○ AUG ○ SEP ○ OCT ○ NOV ○ DEC ○

Creditor:	Debt Type:
Starting Balance:	Credit Limit:
Repayment Frequency:	Interest Rate:
Goal Pay Off Date:	Min Repayment:

DATE	REPAYMENT	BALANCE	NOTES

Expense *Tracker*

JAN ○ FEB ○ MAR ○ APR ○ MAY ○ JUN ○ JUL ○ AUG ○ SEP ○ OCT ○ NOV ○ DEC ○

DATE	DESCRIPTION	AMOUNT	NOTES

TOTAL ______________________

Credit Card *Tracker*

JAN	FEB	MAR	APR	MAY	JUN	JUL	AUG	SEP	OCT	NOV	DEC
○	○	○	○	○	○	○	○	○	○	○	○

DATE	CREDIT CARD	CREDIT LIMIT	%RATE	AMOUNT DUE	AMOUNT PAID	BALANCE

Monthly Financial *Reflection*

JAN ○ FEB ○ MAR ○ APR ○ MAY ○ JUN ○ JUL ○ AUG ○ SEP ○ OCT ○ NOV ○ DEC ○

TOTAL INCOME	TOTAL EXPENSES	DIFFERENCE	BALANCE

Biggest Wins this Month

What am I grateful for?

What do I need to improve for next month?

What did I learn by tracking my finances this month?

Wish *List*

JAN ○ FEB ○ MAR ○ APR ○ MAY ○ JUN ○ JUL ○ AUG ○ SEP ○ OCT ○ NOV ○ DEC ○

WISH LIST	HOPE TO PAY	WHERE TO BUY	BOUGHT	SPENT	SAVED	NOTES
			☐			
			☐			
			☐			
			☐			
			☐			
			☐			
			☐			
			☐			
			☐			
			☐			
			☐			
			☐			
			☐			
			☐			
			☐			
			☐			
			☐			
			☐			
			☐			
			☐			
			☐			
			☐			
			☐			
			☐			

Emergency Fund *Tracker*

JAN ○ FEB ○ MAR ○ APR ○ MAY ○ JUN ○ JUL ○ AUG ○ SEP ○ OCT ○ NOV ○ DEC ○

AMOUNT NEEDED:	TARGET DATE:
MONTHLY SAVINGS TARGET:	ACCOUNT:

Progress Tracker

10%	20%	30%	40%	50%	60%	70%	80%	90%	100%

DATE	DEPOSIT	WITHDRAW	NOTES	BALANCE

Notes

Credit Networking and *Mentorship*

JAN ○ FEB ○ MAR ○ APR ○ MAY ○ JUN ○ JUL ○ AUG ○ SEP ○ OCT ○ NOV ○ DEC ○

Networking Goals

What specific goals do you have for networking this month?

1 ______________________________

2 ______________________________

3 ______________________________

Mentorship Goals

What do you want to achieve with the help of a mentor this month?

1 ______________________________

2 ______________________________

3 ______________________________

Identify Networking Opportunities

Events & Workshops

List credit-related events, workshops, or webinars to attend this month:

1 ______________________________

2 ______________________________

3 ______________________________

Online Communities

Identify online groups or forums where you can engage with others focused on credit improvement:

1 ______________________________

2 ______________________________

3 ______________________________

Track Your Progress

Networking Activities

Record your networking activities for the month (e.g., events attended, new connections made):

1 ______________________________

2 ______________________________

3 ______________________________

Mentorship Activities:

Record your interactions with mentors (e.g., meetings, advice received):

1 ______________________________

2 ______________________________

3 ______________________________

Notes

____

____

____

Charity and *Giving*

JAN ○ FEB ○ MAR ○ APR ○ MAY ○ JUN ○ JUL ○ AUG ○ SEP ○ OCT ○ NOV ○ DEC ○

DONATION	ORGANIZATION	DATE GIVEN	VALUE	TAX DEDUCTIBLE

Self-care and Financial *Health*

JAN ○ FEB ○ MAR ○ APR ○ MAY ○ JUN ○ JUL ○ AUG ○ SEP ○ OCT ○ NOV ○ DEC ○

Self-Care Reflection

- **Physical Well-being**

  What physical health activities will you focus on this month?

  o ______________________________

  o ______________________________

- **Emotional & Mental Wellness**

  What mental health activities will you focus on this month?

  o ______________________________

  o ______________________________

- **Time for Self-Care**

  How will you make time for yourself?

  o ______________________________

  o ______________________________

Financial Health Reflection

- **Current Financial Practices**

  What financial habits do you want to maintain or improve this month?

  o ______________________________

  o ______________________________

- **Financial Goals**

  List your financial goals for this month

  - ______________________________
  - ______________________________

- **Financial Self-Care**

  How will you manage financial stress?

  - ______________________________
  - ______________________________

Accountability & Progress

- **Support System**

  Who will help you stay accountable this month?

  - ______________________________
  - ______________________________

- **Tracking Progress**

  How will you monitor your progress? (e.g., weekly check-ins, journaling)

  - ______________________________
  - ______________________________

- **End-of-Month Review Date**

  Set a date to review your goals and make any necessary adjustments

  - ______________________________

April

SMART Financial Goals *Worksheet*

JAN	FEB	MAR	APR	MAY	JUN	JUL	AUG	SEP	OCT	NOV	DEC
○	○	○	○	○	○	○	○	○	○	○	○

Description of Goals					
SPECIFIC Cost					
MEASURABLE Monthly Amount					
ATTAINABLE Method/Steps					
REALISTIC Goal Length					
TIMEBOUND Your Timeline					

Notes

Monthly Budget *Planner*

JAN ○ FEB ○ MAR ○ APR ○ MAY ○ JUN ○ JUL ○ AUG ○ SEP ○ OCT ○ NOV ○ DEC ○

INCOME	AMOUNT
TOTAL	

BILLS	AMOUNT
TOTAL	

SAVINGS	AMOUNT
TOTAL	

EXPENSES	AMOUNT
TOTAL	

DEBT	AMOUNT
TOTAL	

SUMMARY	AMOUNT
INCOME	
BILLS	
SAVINGS	
EXPENSES	
DEBT	
TOTAL	

Bills Payment *Calendar*

JAN ○ FEB ○ MAR ○ APR ○ MAY ○ JUN ○ JUL ○ AUG ○ SEP ○ OCT ○ NOV ○ DEC ○

SUN	MON	TUE	WED	THU	FRI	SAT
○ ○	○ ○	○ ○	○ ○	○ ○	○ ○	○ ○
○ ○	○ ○	○ ○	○ ○	○ ○	○ ○	○ ○
○ ○	○ ○	○ ○	○ ○	○ ○	○ ○	○ ○
○ ○	○ ○	○ ○	○ ○	○ ○	○ ○	○ ○
○ ○	○ ○	○ ○	○ ○	○ ○	○ ○	○ ○

Debt Repayment *Plan*

JAN ○ FEB ○ MAR ○ APR ○ MAY ○ JUN ○ JUL ○ AUG ○ SEP ○ OCT ○ NOV ○ DEC ○

Creditor:	Debt Type:
Starting Balance:	Credit Limit:
Repayment Frequency:	Interest Rate:
Goal Pay Off Date:	Min Repayment:

DATE	REPAYMENT	BALANCE	NOTES

Expense *Tracker*

JAN ○ FEB ○ MAR ○ APR ○ MAY ○ JUN ○ JUL ○ AUG ○ SEP ○ OCT ○ NOV ○ DEC ○

DATE	DESCRIPTION	AMOUNT	NOTES

TOTAL ____________________

Credit Card *Tracker*

JAN	FEB	MAR	APR	MAY	JUN	JUL	AUG	SEP	OCT	NOV	DEC
○	○	○	○	○	○	○	○	○	○	○	○

DATE	CREDIT CARD	CREDIT LIMIT	%RATE	AMOUNT DUE	AMOUNT PAID	BALANCE

Monthly Financial *Reflection*

JAN ○ FEB ○ MAR ○ APR ○ MAY ○ JUN ○ JUL ○ AUG ○ SEP ○ OCT ○ NOV ○ DEC ○

TOTAL INCOME	TOTAL EXPENSES	DIFFERENCE	BALANCE

Biggest Wins this Month

What am I grateful for?

What do I need to improve for next month?

What did I learn by tracking my finances this month?

Wish *List*

JAN ○ FEB ○ MAR ○ APR ○ MAY ○ JUN ○ JUL ○ AUG ○ SEP ○ OCT ○ NOV ○ DEC ○

WISH LIST	HOPE TO PAY	WHERE TO BUY	BOUGHT	SPENT	SAVED	NOTES
			☐			
			☐			
			☐			
			☐			
			☐			
			☐			
			☐			
			☐			
			☐			
			☐			
			☐			
			☐			
			☐			
			☐			
			☐			
			☐			
			☐			
			☐			
			☐			
			☐			
			☐			
			☐			
			☐			
			☐			

Emergency Fund *Tracker*

JAN ○ FEB ○ MAR ○ APR ○ MAY ○ JUN ○ JUL ○ AUG ○ SEP ○ OCT ○ NOV ○ DEC ○

AMOUNT NEEDED:	TARGET DATE:
MONTHLY SAVINGS TARGET:	ACCOUNT:

Progress Tracker

10%	20%	30%	40%	50%	60%	70%	80%	90%	100%

DATE	DEPOSIT	WITHDRAW	NOTES	BALANCE

Notes

Credit Networking and *Mentorship*

JAN ○ FEB ○ MAR ○ APR ○ MAY ○ JUN ○ JUL ○ AUG ○ SEP ○ OCT ○ NOV ○ DEC ○

Networking Goals

What specific goals do you have for networking this month?

1 ________________________________

2 ________________________________

3 ________________________________

Mentorship Goals

What do you want to achieve with the help of a mentor this month?

1 ________________________________

2 ________________________________

3 ________________________________

Identify Networking Opportunities

Events & Workshops

List credit-related events, workshops, or webinars to attend this month:

1 ________________________________

2 ________________________________

3 ________________________________

Online Communities

Identify online groups or forums where you can engage with others focused on credit improvement:

1 ____________________

2 ____________________

3 ____________________

Track Your Progress

Networking Activities

Record your networking activities for the month (e.g., events attended, new connections made):

1 ____________________

2 ____________________

3 ____________________

Mentorship Activities:

Record your interactions with mentors (e.g., meetings, advice received):

1 ____________________

2 ____________________

3 ____________________

Notes

Charity and *Giving*

JAN ○ FEB ○ MAR ○ APR ○ MAY ○ JUN ○ JUL ○ AUG ○ SEP ○ OCT ○ NOV ○ DEC ○

DONATION	ORGANIZATION	DATE GIVEN	VALUE	TAX DEDUCTIBLE

Self-care and Financial *Health*

JAN ○ FEB ○ MAR ○ APR ○ MAY ○ JUN ○ JUL ○ AUG ○ SEP ○ OCT ○ NOV ○ DEC ○

Self-Care Reflection

- **Physical Well-being**

  What physical health activities will you focus on this month?

  o ______________________________

  o ______________________________

- **Emotional & Mental Wellness**

  What mental health activities will you focus on this month?

  o ______________________________

  o ______________________________

- **Time for Self-Care**

  How will you make time for yourself?

  o ______________________________

  o ______________________________

Financial Health Reflection

- **Current Financial Practices**

  What financial habits do you want to maintain or improve this month?

  o ______________________________

  o ______________________________

- **Financial Goals**

  List your financial goals for this month

  - o ______________________________
  - o ______________________________

- **Financial Self-Care**

  How will you manage financial stress?

  - o ______________________________
  - o ______________________________

Accountability & Progress

- **Support System**

  Who will help you stay accountable this month?

  - o ______________________________
  - o ______________________________

- **Tracking Progress**

  How will you monitor your progress? (e.g., weekly check-ins, journaling)

  - o ______________________________
  - o ______________________________

- **End-of-Month Review Date**

  Set a date to review your goals and make any necessary adjustments

  - o ______________________________

May

SMART Financial Goals *Worksheet*

JAN ○ FEB ○ MAR ○ APR ○ MAY ○ JUN ○ JUL ○ AUG ○ SEP ○ OCT ○ NOV ○ DEC ○

Description of Goals					
SPECIFIC Cost					
MEASURABLE Monthly Amount					
ATTAINABLE Method/Steps					
REALISTIC Goal Length					
TIMEBOUND Your Timeline					

Notes

Monthly Budget *Planner*

JAN ○ FEB ○ MAR ○ APR ○ MAY ○ JUN ○ JUL ○ AUG ○ SEP ○ OCT ○ NOV ○ DEC ○

INCOME	AMOUNT
TOTAL	

BILLS	AMOUNT
TOTAL	

SAVINGS	AMOUNT
TOTAL	

EXPENSES	AMOUNT
TOTAL	

DEBT	AMOUNT
TOTAL	

SUMMARY	AMOUNT
INCOME	
BILLS	
SAVINGS	
EXPENSES	
DEBT	
TOTAL	

Bills Payment *Calendar*

JAN	FEB	MAR	APR	MAY	JUN	JUL	AUG	SEP	OCT	NOV	DEC
○	○	○	○	○	○	○	○	○	○	○	○

SUN	MON	TUE	WED	THU	FRI	SAT

Debt Repayment *Plan*

JAN	FEB	MAR	APR	MAY	JUN	JUL	AUG	SEP	OCT	NOV	DEC
○	○	○	○	○	○	○	○	○	○	○	○

Creditor:	Debt Type:
Starting Balance:	Credit Limit:
Repayment Frequency:	Interest Rate:
Goal Pay Off Date:	Min Repayment:

DATE	REPAYMENT	BALANCE	NOTES

Expense *Tracker*

JAN ○ FEB ○ MAR ○ APR ○ MAY ○ JUN ○ JUL ○ AUG ○ SEP ○ OCT ○ NOV ○ DEC ○

DATE	DESCRIPTION	AMOUNT	NOTES

TOTAL ____________________

Credit Card *Tracker*

JAN ○ FEB ○ MAR ○ APR ○ MAY ○ JUN ○ JUL ○ AUG ○ SEP ○ OCT ○ NOV ○ DEC ○

DATE	CREDIT CARD	CREDIT LIMIT	%RATE	AMOUNT DUE	AMOUNT PAID	BALANCE

Monthly Financial *Reflection*

JAN ○ FEB ○ MAR ○ APR ○ MAY ○ JUN ○ JUL ○ AUG ○ SEP ○ OCT ○ NOV ○ DEC ○

TOTAL INCOME	TOTAL EXPENSES	DIFFERENCE	BALANCE

Biggest Wins this Month

What am I grateful for?

What do I need to improve for next month?

What did I learn by tracking my finances this month?

Wish *List*

JAN	FEB	MAR	APR	MAY	JUN	JUL	AUG	SEP	OCT	NOV	DEC
○	○	○	○	○	○	○	○	○	○	○	○

WISH LIST	HOPE TO PAY	WHERE TO BUY	BOUGHT	SPENT	SAVED	NOTES
			☐			
			☐			
			☐			
			☐			
			☐			
			☐			
			☐			
			☐			
			☐			
			☐			
			☐			
			☐			
			☐			
			☐			
			☐			
			☐			
			☐			
			☐			
			☐			
			☐			
			☐			
			☐			
			☐			
			☐			

Emergency Fund *Tracker*

JAN	FEB	MAR	APR	MAY	JUN	JUL	AUG	SEP	OCT	NOV	DEC
○	○	○	○	○	○	○	○	○	○	○	○

AMOUNT NEEDED:	TARGET DATE:
MONTHLY SAVINGS TARGET:	ACCOUNT:

Progress Tracker

10%	20%	30%	40%	50%	60%	70%	80%	90%	100%

DATE	DEPOSIT	WITHDRAW	NOTES	BALANCE

Notes

Credit Networking and *Mentorship*

JAN ○ FEB ○ MAR ○ APR ○ MAY ○ JUN ○ JUL ○ AUG ○ SEP ○ OCT ○ NOV ○ DEC ○

Networking Goals

What specific goals do you have for networking this month?

1 ______________________________

2 ______________________________

3 ______________________________

Mentorship Goals

What do you want to achieve with the help of a mentor this month?

1 ______________________________

2 ______________________________

3 ______________________________

Identify Networking Opportunities

Events & Workshops

List credit-related events, workshops, or webinars to attend this month:

1 ______________________________

2 ______________________________

3 ______________________________

Online Communities

Identify online groups or forums where you can engage with others focused on credit improvement:

1 ______________________________

2 ______________________________

3 ______________________________

Track Your Progress

Networking Activities

Record your networking activities for the month (e.g., events attended, new connections made):

1 ______________________________

2 ______________________________

3 ______________________________

Mentorship Activities:

Record your interactions with mentors (e.g., meetings, advice received):

1 ______________________________

2 ______________________________

3 ______________________________

Notes

Charity and *Giving*

JAN ○ FEB ○ MAR ○ APR ○ MAY ○ JUN ○ JUL ○ AUG ○ SEP ○ OCT ○ NOV ○ DEC ○

DONATION	ORGANIZATION	DATE GIVEN	VALUE	TAX DEDUCTIBLE

Self-care and Financial *Health*

JAN FEB MAR APR MAY JUN JUL AUG SEP OCT NOV DEC
○ ○ ○ ○ ○ ○ ○ ○ ○ ○ ○ ○

Self-Care Reflection

- **Physical Well-being**

  What physical health activities will you focus on this month?

  o ______________________________

  o ______________________________

- **Emotional & Mental Wellness**

  What mental health activities will you focus on this month?

  o ______________________________

  o ______________________________

- **Time for Self-Care**

  How will you make time for yourself?

  o ______________________________

  o ______________________________

Financial Health Reflection

- **Current Financial Practices**

  What financial habits do you want to maintain or improve this month?

  o ______________________________

  o ______________________________

- **Financial Goals**

  List your financial goals for this month

  - o ______________________________
  - o ______________________________

- **Financial Self-Care**

  How will you manage financial stress?

  - o ______________________________
  - o ______________________________

Accountability & Progress

- **Support System**

  Who will help you stay accountable this month?

  - o ______________________________
  - o ______________________________

- **Tracking Progress**

  How will you monitor your progress? (e.g., weekly check-ins, journaling)

  - o ______________________________
  - o ______________________________

- **End-of-Month Review Date**

  Set a date to review your goals and make any necessary adjustments

  - o ______________________________

June

SMART Financial Goals *Worksheet*

JAN ○ FEB ○ MAR ○ APR ○ MAY ○ JUN ○ JUL ○ AUG ○ SEP ○ OCT ○ NOV ○ DEC ○

Description of Goals					
SPECIFIC Cost					
MEASURABLE Monthly Amount					
ATTAINABLE Method/Steps					
REALISTIC Goal Length					
TIMEBOUND Your Timeline					

Notes

Monthly Budget *Planner*

JAN ○ FEB ○ MAR ○ APR ○ MAY ○ JUN ○ JUL ○ AUG ○ SEP ○ OCT ○ NOV ○ DEC ○

INCOME	AMOUNT
TOTAL	

BILLS	AMOUNT
TOTAL	

SAVINGS	AMOUNT
TOTAL	

EXPENSES	AMOUNT
TOTAL	

DEBT	AMOUNT
TOTAL	

SUMMARY	AMOUNT
INCOME	
BILLS	
SAVINGS	
EXPENSES	
DEBT	
TOTAL	

Bills Payment *Calendar*

JAN ○ FEB ○ MAR ○ APR ○ MAY ○ JUN ○ JUL ○ AUG ○ SEP ○ OCT ○ NOV ○ DEC ○

SUN	MON	TUE	WED	THU	FRI	SAT
○ ○	○ ○	○ ○	○ ○	○ ○	○ ○	○ ○
○ ○	○ ○	○ ○	○ ○	○ ○	○ ○	○ ○
○ ○	○ ○	○ ○	○ ○	○ ○	○ ○	○ ○
○ ○	○ ○	○ ○	○ ○	○ ○	○ ○	○ ○
○ ○	○ ○	○ ○	○ ○	○ ○	○ ○	○ ○

Debt Repayment *Plan*

JAN ○ FEB ○ MAR ○ APR ○ MAY ○ JUN ○ JUL ○ AUG ○ SEP ○ OCT ○ NOV ○ DEC ○

Creditor:	Debt Type:
Starting Balance:	Credit Limit:
Repayment Frequency:	Interest Rate:
Goal Pay Off Date:	Min Repayment:

DATE	REPAYMENT	BALANCE	NOTES

Expense *Tracker*

JAN ○ FEB ○ MAR ○ APR ○ MAY ○ JUN ○ JUL ○ AUG ○ SEP ○ OCT ○ NOV ○ DEC ○

DATE	DESCRIPTION	AMOUNT	NOTES

TOTAL ______________________

Credit Card *Tracker*

JAN	FEB	MAR	APR	MAY	JUN	JUL	AUG	SEP	OCT	NOV	DEC
○	○	○	○	○	○	○	○	○	○	○	○

DATE	CREDIT CARD	CREDIT LIMIT	%RATE	AMOUNT DUE	AMOUNT PAID	BALANCE

Monthly Financial *Reflection*

JAN ○ FEB ○ MAR ○ APR ○ MAY ○ JUN ○ JUL ○ AUG ○ SEP ○ OCT ○ NOV ○ DEC ○

TOTAL INCOME	TOTAL EXPENSES	DIFFERENCE	BALANCE

Biggest Wins this Month

What am I grateful for?

What do I need to improve for next month?

What did I learn by tracking my finances this month?

Wish *List*

JAN	FEB	MAR	APR	MAY	JUN	JUL	AUG	SEP	OCT	NOV	DEC
○	○	○	○	○	○	○	○	○	○	○	○

WISH LIST	HOPE TO PAY	WHERE TO BUY	BOUGHT	SPENT	SAVED	NOTES
			☐			
			☐			
			☐			
			☐			
			☐			
			☐			
			☐			
			☐			
			☐			
			☐			
			☐			
			☐			
			☐			
			☐			
			☐			
			☐			
			☐			
			☐			
			☐			
			☐			
			☐			
			☐			
			☐			
			☐			

Emergency Fund *Tracker*

JAN ○ FEB ○ MAR ○ APR ○ MAY ○ JUN ○ JUL ○ AUG ○ SEP ○ OCT ○ NOV ○ DEC ○

AMOUNT NEEDED:	TARGET DATE:
MONTHLY SAVINGS TARGET:	ACCOUNT:

Progress Tracker

10%	20%	30%	40%	50%	60%	70%	80%	90%	100%

DATE	DEPOSIT	WITHDRAW	NOTES	BALANCE

Notes

Credit Networking and *Mentorship*

JAN	FEB	MAR	APR	MAY	JUN	JUL	AUG	SEP	OCT	NOV	DEC
○	○	○	○	○	○	○	○	○	○	○	○

Networking Goals

What specific goals do you have for networking this month?

1 ______________________________

2 ______________________________

3 ______________________________

Mentorship Goals

What do you want to achieve with the help of a mentor this month?

1 ______________________________

2 ______________________________

3 ______________________________

Identify Networking Opportunities

Events & Workshops

List credit-related events, workshops, or webinars to attend this month:

1 ______________________________

2 ______________________________

3 ______________________________

Online Communities

Identify online groups or forums where you can engage with others focused on credit improvement:

1 ______________________________

2 ______________________________

3 ______________________________

Track Your Progress

Networking Activities

Record your networking activities for the month (e.g., events attended, new connections made):

1 ______________________________

2 ______________________________

3 ______________________________

Mentorship Activities:

Record your interactions with mentors (e.g., meetings, advice received):

1 ______________________________

2 ______________________________

3 ______________________________

Notes

____

____

____

Charity and *Giving*

JAN ○ FEB ○ MAR ○ APR ○ MAY ○ JUN ○ JUL ○ AUG ○ SEP ○ OCT ○ NOV ○ DEC ○

DONATION	ORGANIZATION	DATE GIVEN	VALUE	TAX DEDUCTIBLE

Self-care and Financial *Health*

JAN ○ FEB ○ MAR ○ APR ○ MAY ○ JUN ○ JUL ○ AUG ○ SEP ○ OCT ○ NOV ○ DEC ○

Self-Care Reflection

- **Physical Well-being**

  What physical health activities will you focus on this month?

  o ______________________________

  o ______________________________

- **Emotional & Mental Wellness**

  What mental health activities will you focus on this month?

  o ______________________________

  o ______________________________

- **Time for Self-Care**

  How will you make time for yourself?

  o ______________________________

  o ______________________________

Financial Health Reflection

- **Current Financial Practices**

  What financial habits do you want to maintain or improve this month?

  o ______________________________

  o ______________________________

- **Financial Goals**

  List your financial goals for this month

  - o ______________________________
  - o ______________________________

- **Financial Self-Care**

  How will you manage financial stress?

  - o ______________________________
  - o ______________________________

Accountability & Progress

- **Support System**

  Who will help you stay accountable this month?

  - o ______________________________
  - o ______________________________

- **Tracking Progress**

  How will you monitor your progress? (e.g., weekly check-ins, journaling)

  - o ______________________________
  - o ______________________________

- **End-of-Month Review Date**

  Set a date to review your goals and make any necessary adjustments

  - o ______________________________

July

SMART Financial Goals *Worksheet*

JAN ○ FEB ○ MAR ○ APR ○ MAY ○ JUN ○ JUL ○ AUG ○ SEP ○ OCT ○ NOV ○ DEC ○

Description of Goals					
SPECIFIC Cost					
MEASURABLE Monthly Amount					
ATTAINABLE Method/Steps					
REALISTIC Goal Length					
TIMEBOUND Your Timeline					

Notes

Monthly Budget *Planner*

JAN ○ FEB ○ MAR ○ APR ○ MAY ○ JUN ○ JUL ○ AUG ○ SEP ○ OCT ○ NOV ○ DEC ○

INCOME	AMOUNT
TOTAL	

BILLS	AMOUNT
TOTAL	

SAVINGS	AMOUNT
TOTAL	

EXPENSES	AMOUNT
TOTAL	

DEBT	AMOUNT
TOTAL	

SUMMARY	AMOUNT
INCOME	
BILLS	
SAVINGS	
EXPENSES	
DEBT	
TOTAL	

Bills Payment *Calendar*

JAN ○ FEB ○ MAR ○ APR ○ MAY ○ JUN ○ JUL ○ AUG ○ SEP ○ OCT ○ NOV ○ DEC ○

SUN	MON	TUE	WED	THU	FRI	SAT
○ ○	○ ○	○ ○	○ ○	○ ○	○ ○	○ ○
○ ○	○ ○	○ ○	○ ○	○ ○	○ ○	○ ○
○ ○	○ ○	○ ○	○ ○	○ ○	○ ○	○ ○
○ ○	○ ○	○ ○	○ ○	○ ○	○ ○	○ ○
○ ○	○ ○	○ ○	○ ○	○ ○	○ ○	○ ○

Debt Repayment *Plan*

JAN ○ FEB ○ MAR ○ APR ○ MAY ○ JUN ○ JUL ○ AUG ○ SEP ○ OCT ○ NOV ○ DEC ○

Creditor:	Debt Type:
Starting Balance:	Credit Limit:
Repayment Frequency:	Interest Rate:
Goal Pay Off Date:	Min Repayment:

DATE	REPAYMENT	BALANCE	NOTES

Expense *Tracker*

JAN ○ FEB ○ MAR ○ APR ○ MAY ○ JUN ○ JUL ○ AUG ○ SEP ○ OCT ○ NOV ○ DEC ○

DATE	DESCRIPTION	AMOUNT	NOTES

TOTAL ____________________

Credit Card *Tracker*

JAN ○ FEB ○ MAR ○ APR ○ MAY ○ JUN ○ JUL ○ AUG ○ SEP ○ OCT ○ NOV ○ DEC ○

DATE	CREDIT CARD	CREDIT LIMIT	%RATE	AMOUNT DUE	AMOUNT PAID	BALANCE

Monthly Financial *Reflection*

JAN ○ FEB ○ MAR ○ APR ○ MAY ○ JUN ○ JUL ○ AUG ○ SEP ○ OCT ○ NOV ○ DEC ○

TOTAL INCOME	TOTAL EXPENSES	DIFFERENCE	BALANCE

Biggest Wins this Month

What am I grateful for?

What do I need to improve for next month?

What did I learn by tracking my finances this month?

Wish *List*

JAN ○ FEB ○ MAR ○ APR ○ MAY ○ JUN ○ JUL ○ AUG ○ SEP ○ OCT ○ NOV ○ DEC ○

WISH LIST	HOPE TO PAY	WHERE TO BUY	BOUGHT	SPENT	SAVED	NOTES
			☐			
			☐			
			☐			
			☐			
			☐			
			☐			
			☐			
			☐			
			☐			
			☐			
			☐			
			☐			
			☐			
			☐			
			☐			
			☐			
			☐			
			☐			
			☐			
			☐			
			☐			
			☐			
			☐			
			☐			

Emergency Fund *Tracker*

JAN ○ FEB ○ MAR ○ APR ○ MAY ○ JUN ○ JUL ○ AUG ○ SEP ○ OCT ○ NOV ○ DEC ○

AMOUNT NEEDED:	TARGET DATE:
MONTHLY SAVINGS TARGET:	ACCOUNT:

Progress Tracker

10%	20%	30%	40%	50%	60%	70%	80%	90%	100%

DATE	DEPOSIT	WITHDRAW	NOTES	BALANCE

Notes

Credit Networking and *Mentorship*

JAN ○ FEB ○ MAR ○ APR ○ MAY ○ JUN ○ JUL ○ AUG ○ SEP ○ OCT ○ NOV ○ DEC ○

Networking Goals

What specific goals do you have for networking this month?

1 ____

2 ____

3 ____

Mentorship Goals

What do you want to achieve with the help of a mentor this month?

1 ____

2 ____

3 ____

Identify Networking Opportunities

Events & Workshops

List credit-related events, workshops, or webinars to attend this month:

1 ____

2 ____

3 ____

Online Communities

Identify online groups or forums where you can engage with others focused on credit improvement:

1 ___

2 ___

3 ___

Track Your Progress

Networking Activities

Record your networking activities for the month (e.g., events attended, new connections made):

1 ___

2 ___

3 ___

Mentorship Activities:

Record your interactions with mentors (e.g., meetings, advice received):

1 ___

2 ___

3 ___

Notes

___

___

___

Charity and *Giving*

JAN	FEB	MAR	APR	MAY	JUN	JUL	AUG	SEP	OCT	NOV	DEC
○	○	○	○	○	○	○	○	○	○	○	○

DONATION	ORGANIZATION	DATE GIVEN	VALUE	TAX DEDUCTIBLE

Self-care and Financial *Health*

JAN ○ FEB ○ MAR ○ APR ○ MAY ○ JUN ○ JUL ○ AUG ○ SEP ○ OCT ○ NOV ○ DEC ○

Self-Care Reflection

- **Physical Well-being**

  What physical health activities will you focus on this month?

  o ______

  o ______

- **Emotional & Mental Wellness**

  What mental health activities will you focus on this month?

  o ______

  o ______

- **Time for Self-Care**

  How will you make time for yourself?

  o ______

  o ______

Financial Health Reflection

- **Current Financial Practices**

  What financial habits do you want to maintain or improve this month?

  o ______

  o ______

- **Financial Goals**

  List your financial goals for this month

  - o ______________________________
  - o ______________________________

- **Financial Self-Care**

  How will you manage financial stress?

  - o ______________________________
  - o ______________________________

Accountability & Progress

- **Support System**

  Who will help you stay accountable this month?

  - o ______________________________
  - o ______________________________

- **Tracking Progress**

  How will you monitor your progress? (e.g., weekly check-ins, journaling)

  - o ______________________________
  - o ______________________________

- **End-of-Month Review Date**

  Set a date to review your goals and make any necessary adjustments

  - o ______________________________

August

SMART Financial Goals *Worksheet*

JAN ○ FEB ○ MAR ○ APR ○ MAY ○ JUN ○ JUL ○ AUG ○ SEP ○ OCT ○ NOV ○ DEC ○

Description of Goals					
SPECIFIC Cost					
MEASURABLE Monthly Amount					
ATTAINABLE Method/Steps					
REALISTIC Goal Length					
TIMEBOUND Your Timeline					

Notes

Monthly Budget *Planner*

JAN ○ FEB ○ MAR ○ APR ○ MAY ○ JUN ○ JUL ○ AUG ○ SEP ○ OCT ○ NOV ○ DEC ○

INCOME	AMOUNT
TOTAL	

EXPENSES	AMOUNT
TOTAL	

BILLS	AMOUNT
TOTAL	

DEBT	AMOUNT
TOTAL	

SAVINGS	AMOUNT
TOTAL	

SUMMARY	AMOUNT
INCOME	
BILLS	
SAVINGS	
EXPENSES	
DEBT	
TOTAL	

Bills Payment *Calendar*

JAN	FEB	MAR	APR	MAY	JUN	JUL	AUG	SEP	OCT	NOV	DEC
○	○	○	○	○	○	○	○	○	○	○	○

SUN	MON	TUE	WED	THU	FRI	SAT
○ ○	○ ○	○ ○	○ ○	○ ○	○ ○	○ ○
○ ○	○ ○	○ ○	○ ○	○ ○	○ ○	○ ○
○ ○	○ ○	○ ○	○ ○	○ ○	○ ○	○ ○
○ ○	○ ○	○ ○	○ ○	○ ○	○ ○	○ ○
○ ○	○ ○	○ ○	○ ○	○ ○	○ ○	○ ○

Debt Repayment *Plan*

JAN	FEB	MAR	APR	MAY	JUN	JUL	AUG	SEP	OCT	NOV	DEC
○	○	○	○	○	○	○	○	○	○	○	○

Creditor:	Debt Type:
Starting Balance:	Credit Limit:
Repayment Frequency:	Interest Rate:
Goal Pay Off Date:	Min Repayment:

DATE	REPAYMENT	BALANCE	NOTES

Expense *Tracker*

JAN ○ FEB ○ MAR ○ APR ○ MAY ○ JUN ○ JUL ○ AUG ○ SEP ○ OCT ○ NOV ○ DEC ○

DATE	DESCRIPTION	AMOUNT	NOTES

TOTAL ____________________

Credit Card *Tracker*

JAN ○ FEB ○ MAR ○ APR ○ MAY ○ JUN ○ JUL ○ AUG ○ SEP ○ OCT ○ NOV ○ DEC ○

DATE	CREDIT CARD	CREDIT LIMIT	%RATE	AMOUNT DUE	AMOUNT PAID	BALANCE

Monthly Financial *Reflection*

JAN ○ FEB ○ MAR ○ APR ○ MAY ○ JUN ○ JUL ○ AUG ○ SEP ○ OCT ○ NOV ○ DEC ○

TOTAL INCOME	TOTAL EXPENSES	DIFFERENCE	BALANCE

Biggest Wins this Month

What am I grateful for?

What do I need to improve for next month?

What did I learn by tracking my finances this month?

Wish *List*

JAN	FEB	MAR	APR	MAY	JUN	JUL	AUG	SEP	OCT	NOV	DEC
○	○	○	○	○	○	○	○	○	○	○	○

WISH LIST	HOPE TO PAY	WHERE TO BUY	BOUGHT	SPENT	SAVED	NOTES
			☐			
			☐			
			☐			
			☐			
			☐			
			☐			
			☐			
			☐			
			☐			
			☐			
			☐			
			☐			
			☐			
			☐			
			☐			
			☐			
			☐			
			☐			
			☐			
			☐			
			☐			
			☐			
			☐			
			☐			

Emergency Fund *Tracker*

JAN ○ FEB ○ MAR ○ APR ○ MAY ○ JUN ○ JUL ○ AUG ○ SEP ○ OCT ○ NOV ○ DEC ○

AMOUNT NEEDED:	TARGET DATE:
MONTHLY SAVINGS TARGET:	ACCOUNT:

Progress Tracker

10%	20%	30%	40%	50%	60%	70%	80%	90%	100%

DATE	DEPOSIT	WITHDRAW	NOTES	BALANCE

Notes

Credit Networking and *Mentorship*

JAN ○ FEB ○ MAR ○ APR ○ MAY ○ JUN ○ JUL ○ AUG ○ SEP ○ OCT ○ NOV ○ DEC ○

Networking Goals

What specific goals do you have for networking this month?

1 ______________________________

2 ______________________________

3 ______________________________

Mentorship Goals

What do you want to achieve with the help of a mentor this month?

1 ______________________________

2 ______________________________

3 ______________________________

Identify Networking Opportunities

Events & Workshops

List credit-related events, workshops, or webinars to attend this month:

1 ______________________________

2 ______________________________

3 ______________________________

Online Communities

Identify online groups or forums where you can engage with others focused on credit improvement:

1 ______

2 ______

3 ______

Track Your Progress

Networking Activities

Record your networking activities for the month (e.g., events attended, new connections made):

1 ______

2 ______

3 ______

Mentorship Activities:

Record your interactions with mentors (e.g., meetings, advice received):

1 ______

2 ______

3 ______

Notes

______

______

______

Charity and *Giving*

JAN ○ FEB ○ MAR ○ APR ○ MAY ○ JUN ○ JUL ○ AUG ○ SEP ○ OCT ○ NOV ○ DEC ○

DONATION	ORGANIZATION	DATE GIVEN	VALUE	TAX DEDUCTIBLE

Self-care and Financial *Health*

JAN ○ FEB ○ MAR ○ APR ○ MAY ○ JUN ○ JUL ○ AUG ○ SEP ○ OCT ○ NOV ○ DEC ○

Self-Care Reflection

- **Physical Well-being**

  What physical health activities will you focus on this month?

  o ______________________________

  o ______________________________

- **Emotional & Mental Wellness**

  What mental health activities will you focus on this month?

  o ______________________________

  o ______________________________

- **Time for Self-Care**

  How will you make time for yourself?

  o ______________________________

  o ______________________________

Financial Health Reflection

- **Current Financial Practices**

  What financial habits do you want to maintain or improve this month?

  o ______________________________

  o ______________________________

- **Financial Goals**

  List your financial goals for this month

  - ______________________________
  - ______________________________

- **Financial Self-Care**

  How will you manage financial stress?

  - ______________________________
  - ______________________________

Accountability & Progress

- **Support System**

  Who will help you stay accountable this month?

  - ______________________________
  - ______________________________

- **Tracking Progress**

  How will you monitor your progress? (e.g., weekly check-ins, journaling)

  - ______________________________
  - ______________________________

- **End-of-Month Review Date**

  Set a date to review your goals and make any necessary adjustments

  - ______________________________

September

SMART Financial Goals *Worksheet*

JAN ○ FEB ○ MAR ○ APR ○ MAY ○ JUN ○ JUL ○ AUG ○ SEP ○ OCT ○ NOV ○ DEC ○

Description of Goals					
SPECIFIC Cost					
MEASURABLE Monthly Amount					
ATTAINABLE Method/Steps					
REALISTIC Goal Length					
TIMEBOUND Your Timeline					

Notes

Monthly Budget *Planner*

JAN ○ FEB ○ MAR ○ APR ○ MAY ○ JUN ○ JUL ○ AUG ○ SEP ○ OCT ○ NOV ○ DEC ○

INCOME	AMOUNT
TOTAL	

EXPENSES	AMOUNT
TOTAL	

BILLS	AMOUNT
TOTAL	

DEBT	AMOUNT
TOTAL	

SAVINGS	AMOUNT
TOTAL	

SUMMARY	AMOUNT
INCOME	
BILLS	
SAVINGS	
EXPENSES	
DEBT	
TOTAL	

Bills Payment *Calendar*

JAN ○ FEB ○ MAR ○ APR ○ MAY ○ JUN ○ JUL ○ AUG ○ SEP ○ OCT ○ NOV ○ DEC ○

SUN	MON	TUE	WED	THU	FRI	SAT

Debt Repayment *Plan*

JAN ○ FEB ○ MAR ○ APR ○ MAY ○ JUN ○ JUL ○ AUG ○ SEP ○ OCT ○ NOV ○ DEC ○

Creditor:	Debt Type:
Starting Balance:	Credit Limit:
Repayment Frequency:	Interest Rate:
Goal Pay Off Date:	Min Repayment:

DATE	REPAYMENT	BALANCE	NOTES

Expense *Tracker*

JAN ○ FEB ○ MAR ○ APR ○ MAY ○ JUN ○ JUL ○ AUG ○ SEP ○ OCT ○ NOV ○ DEC ○

DATE	DESCRIPTION	AMOUNT	NOTES

TOTAL ______________________

Credit Card *Tracker*

JAN ○ FEB ○ MAR ○ APR ○ MAY ○ JUN ○ JUL ○ AUG ○ SEP ○ OCT ○ NOV ○ DEC ○

DATE	CREDIT CARD	CREDIT LIMIT	%RATE	AMOUNT DUE	AMOUNT PAID	BALANCE

Monthly Financial *Reflection*

JAN ○ FEB ○ MAR ○ APR ○ MAY ○ JUN ○ JUL ○ AUG ○ SEP ○ OCT ○ NOV ○ DEC ○

TOTAL INCOME	TOTAL EXPENSES	DIFFERENCE	BALANCE

Biggest Wins this Month

What am I grateful for?

What do I need to improve for next month?

What did I learn by tracking my finances this month?

Wish *List*

JAN ○ FEB ○ MAR ○ APR ○ MAY ○ JUN ○ JUL ○ AUG ○ SEP ○ OCT ○ NOV ○ DEC ○

WISH LIST	HOPE TO PAY	WHERE TO BUY	BOUGHT	SPENT	SAVED	NOTES
			☐			
			☐			
			☐			
			☐			
			☐			
			☐			
			☐			
			☐			
			☐			
			☐			
			☐			
			☐			
			☐			
			☐			
			☐			
			☐			
			☐			
			☐			
			☐			
			☐			
			☐			
			☐			
			☐			
			☐			

Emergency Fund Tracker

JAN ○ FEB ○ MAR ○ APR ○ MAY ○ JUN ○ JUL ○ AUG ○ SEP ○ OCT ○ NOV ○ DEC ○

AMOUNT NEEDED:	TARGET DATE:
MONTHLY SAVINGS TARGET:	ACCOUNT:

Progress Tracker

10%	20%	30%	40%	50%	60%	70%	80%	90%	100%

DATE	DEPOSIT	WITHDRAW	NOTES	BALANCE

Notes

Credit Networking and *Mentorship*

JAN ○ FEB ○ MAR ○ APR ○ MAY ○ JUN ○ JUL ○ AUG ○ SEP ○ OCT ○ NOV ○ DEC ○

Networking Goals

What specific goals do you have for networking this month?

1 ______________________________

2 ______________________________

3 ______________________________

Mentorship Goals

What do you want to achieve with the help of a mentor this month?

1 ______________________________

2 ______________________________

3 ______________________________

Identify Networking Opportunities

Events & Workshops

List credit-related events, workshops, or webinars to attend this month:

1 ______________________________

2 ______________________________

3 ______________________________

Online Communities

Identify online groups or forums where you can engage with others focused on credit improvement:

1 ______

2 ______

3 ______

Track Your Progress

Networking Activities

Record your networking activities for the month (e.g., events attended, new connections made):

1 ______

2 ______

3 ______

Mentorship Activities:

Record your interactions with mentors (e.g., meetings, advice received):

1 ______

2 ______

3 ______

Notes

______

______

______

Charity and *Giving*

JAN ○ FEB ○ MAR ○ APR ○ MAY ○ JUN ○ JUL ○ AUG ○ SEP ○ OCT ○ NOV ○ DEC ○

DONATION	ORGANIZATION	DATE GIVEN	VALUE	TAX DEDUCTIBLE

Self-care and Financial *Health*

JAN ○ FEB ○ MAR ○ APR ○ MAY ○ JUN ○ JUL ○ AUG ○ SEP ○ OCT ○ NOV ○ DEC ○

Self-Care Reflection

- **Physical Well-being**

  What physical health activities will you focus on this month?

  o ______________________________

  o ______________________________

- **Emotional & Mental Wellness**

  What mental health activities will you focus on this month?

  o ______________________________

  o ______________________________

- **Time for Self-Care**

  How will you make time for yourself?

  o ______________________________

  o ______________________________

Financial Health Reflection

- **Current Financial Practices**

  What financial habits do you want to maintain or improve this month?

  o ______________________________

  o ______________________________

- **Financial Goals**

  List your financial goals for this month

  - o ______________________________
  - o ______________________________

- **Financial Self-Care**

  How will you manage financial stress?

  - o ______________________________
  - o ______________________________

Accountability & Progress

- **Support System**

  Who will help you stay accountable this month?

  - o ______________________________
  - o ______________________________

- **Tracking Progress**

  How will you monitor your progress? (e.g., weekly check-ins, journaling)

  - o ______________________________
  - o ______________________________

- **End-of-Month Review Date**

  Set a date to review your goals and make any necessary adjustments

  - o ______________________________

October

SMART Financial Goals *Worksheet*

JAN ○ FEB ○ MAR ○ APR ○ MAY ○ JUN ○ JUL ○ AUG ○ SEP ○ OCT ○ NOV ○ DEC ○

Description of Goals					
SPECIFIC Cost					
MEASURABLE Monthly Amount					
ATTAINABLE Method/Steps					
REALISTIC Goal Length					
TIMEBOUND Your Timeline					

Notes

Monthly Budget *Planner*

JAN ○ FEB ○ MAR ○ APR ○ MAY ○ JUN ○ JUL ○ AUG ○ SEP ○ OCT ○ NOV ○ DEC ○

INCOME	AMOUNT
TOTAL	

EXPENSES	AMOUNT
TOTAL	

BILLS	AMOUNT
TOTAL	

DEBT	AMOUNT
TOTAL	

SAVINGS	AMOUNT
TOTAL	

SUMMARY	AMOUNT
INCOME	
BILLS	
SAVINGS	
EXPENSES	
DEBT	
TOTAL	

Bills Payment *Calendar*

JAN ○ FEB ○ MAR ○ APR ○ MAY ○ JUN ○ JUL ○ AUG ○ SEP ○ OCT ○ NOV ○ DEC ○

SUN	MON	TUE	WED	THU	FRI	SAT
○ ○	○ ○	○ ○	○ ○	○ ○	○ ○	○ ○
○ ○	○ ○	○ ○	○ ○	○ ○	○ ○	○ ○
○ ○	○ ○	○ ○	○ ○	○ ○	○ ○	○ ○
○ ○	○ ○	○ ○	○ ○	○ ○	○ ○	○ ○
○ ○	○ ○	○ ○	○ ○	○ ○	○ ○	○ ○

Debt Repayment *Plan*

JAN ○ FEB ○ MAR ○ APR ○ MAY ○ JUN ○ JUL ○ AUG ○ SEP ○ OCT ○ NOV ○ DEC ○

Creditor:	Debt Type:
Starting Balance:	Credit Limit:
Repayment Frequency:	Interest Rate:
Goal Pay Off Date:	Min Repayment:

DATE	REPAYMENT	BALANCE	NOTES

Expense *Tracker*

JAN ○ FEB ○ MAR ○ APR ○ MAY ○ JUN ○ JUL ○ AUG ○ SEP ○ OCT ○ NOV ○ DEC ○

DATE	DESCRIPTION	AMOUNT	NOTES

TOTAL ______________________

Credit Card *Tracker*

JAN ○ FEB ○ MAR ○ APR ○ MAY ○ JUN ○ JUL ○ AUG ○ SEP ○ OCT ○ NOV ○ DEC ○

DATE	CREDIT CARD	CREDIT LIMIT	%RATE	AMOUNT DUE	AMOUNT PAID	BALANCE

Monthly Financial *Reflection*

JAN ○ FEB ○ MAR ○ APR ○ MAY ○ JUN ○ JUL ○ AUG ○ SEP ○ OCT ○ NOV ○ DEC ○

TOTAL INCOME	TOTAL EXPENSES	DIFFERENCE	BALANCE

Biggest Wins this Month

What am I grateful for?

What do I need to improve for next month?

What did I learn by tracking my finances this month?

Wish *List*

JAN	FEB	MAR	APR	MAY	JUN	JUL	AUG	SEP	OCT	NOV	DEC
○	○	○	○	○	○	○	○	○	○	○	○

WISH LIST	HOPE TO PAY	WHERE TO BUY	BOUGHT	SPENT	SAVED	NOTES
			☐			
			☐			
			☐			
			☐			
			☐			
			☐			
			☐			
			☐			
			☐			
			☐			
			☐			
			☐			
			☐			
			☐			
			☐			
			☐			
			☐			
			☐			
			☐			
			☐			
			☐			
			☐			
			☐			
			☐			

Emergency Fund Tracker

JAN ○ FEB ○ MAR ○ APR ○ MAY ○ JUN ○ JUL ○ AUG ○ SEP ○ OCT ○ NOV ○ DEC ○

AMOUNT NEEDED:	TARGET DATE:
MONTHLY SAVINGS TARGET:	ACCOUNT:

Progress Tracker

10%	20%	30%	40%	50%	60%	70%	80%	90%	100%

DATE	DEPOSIT	WITHDRAW	NOTES	BALANCE

Notes

Credit Networking and *Mentorship*

JAN ○ FEB ○ MAR ○ APR ○ MAY ○ JUN ○ JUL ○ AUG ○ SEP ○ OCT ○ NOV ○ DEC ○

Networking Goals

What specific goals do you have for networking this month?

1 ________________________

2 ________________________

3 ________________________

Mentorship Goals

What do you want to achieve with the help of a mentor this month?

1 ________________________

2 ________________________

3 ________________________

Identify Networking Opportunities

Events & Workshops

List credit-related events, workshops, or webinars to attend this month:

1 ________________________

2 ________________________

3 ________________________

Online Communities

Identify online groups or forums where you can engage with others focused on credit improvement:

1 ____________________

2 ____________________

3 ____________________

Track Your Progress

Networking Activities

Record your networking activities for the month (e.g., events attended, new connections made):

1 ____________________

2 ____________________

3 ____________________

Mentorship Activities:

Record your interactions with mentors (e.g., meetings, advice received):

1 ____________________

2 ____________________

3 ____________________

Notes

Charity and *Giving*

JAN ○ FEB ○ MAR ○ APR ○ MAY ○ JUN ○ JUL ○ AUG ○ SEP ○ OCT ○ NOV ○ DEC ○

DONATION	ORGANIZATION	DATE GIVEN	VALUE	TAX DEDUCTIBLE

Self-care and Financial *Health*

JAN ○ FEB ○ MAR ○ APR ○ MAY ○ JUN ○ JUL ○ AUG ○ SEP ○ OCT ○ NOV ○ DEC ○

Self-Care Reflection

- **Physical Well-being**

  What physical health activities will you focus on this month?

  o ______________________________

  o ______________________________

- **Emotional & Mental Wellness**

  What mental health activities will you focus on this month?

  o ______________________________

  o ______________________________

- **Time for Self-Care**

  How will you make time for yourself?

  o ______________________________

  o ______________________________

Financial Health Reflection

- **Current Financial Practices**

  What financial habits do you want to maintain or improve this month?

  o ______________________________

  o ______________________________

- **Financial Goals**

  List your financial goals for this month

  - o ____________________
  - o ____________________

- **Financial Self-Care**

  How will you manage financial stress?

  - o ____________________
  - o ____________________

Accountability & Progress

- **Support System**

  Who will help you stay accountable this month?

  - o ____________________
  - o ____________________

- **Tracking Progress**

  How will you monitor your progress? (e.g., weekly check-ins, journaling)

  - o ____________________
  - o ____________________

- **End-of-Month Review Date**

  Set a date to review your goals and make any necessary adjustments

  - o ____________________

November

SMART Financial Goals *Worksheet*

JAN ○ FEB ○ MAR ○ APR ○ MAY ○ JUN ○ JUL ○ AUG ○ SEP ○ OCT ○ NOV ○ DEC ○

Description of Goals					
SPECIFIC Cost					
MEASURABLE Monthly Amount					
ATTAINABLE Method/Steps					
REALISTIC Goal Length					
TIMEBOUND Your Timeline					

Notes

Monthly Budget *Planner*

JAN ○ FEB ○ MAR ○ APR ○ MAY ○ JUN ○ JUL ○ AUG ○ SEP ○ OCT ○ NOV ○ DEC ○

INCOME	AMOUNT
TOTAL	

BILLS	AMOUNT
TOTAL	

SAVINGS	AMOUNT
TOTAL	

EXPENSES	AMOUNT
TOTAL	

DEBT	AMOUNT
TOTAL	

SUMMARY	AMOUNT
INCOME	
BILLS	
SAVINGS	
EXPENSES	
DEBT	
TOTAL	

Bills Payment *Calendar*

JAN ○ FEB ○ MAR ○ APR ○ MAY ○ JUN ○ JUL ○ AUG ○ SEP ○ OCT ○ NOV ○ DEC ○

SUN	MON	TUE	WED	THU	FRI	SAT
○ ○	○ ○	○ ○	○ ○	○ ○	○ ○	○ ○
○ ○	○ ○	○ ○	○ ○	○ ○	○ ○	○ ○
○ ○	○ ○	○ ○	○ ○	○ ○	○ ○	○ ○
○ ○	○ ○	○ ○	○ ○	○ ○	○ ○	○ ○
○ ○	○ ○	○ ○	○ ○	○ ○	○ ○	○ ○

Debt Repayment *Plan*

JAN ○ FEB ○ MAR ○ APR ○ MAY ○ JUN ○ JUL ○ AUG ○ SEP ○ OCT ○ NOV ○ DEC ○

Creditor:	Debt Type:
Starting Balance:	Credit Limit:
Repayment Frequency:	Interest Rate:
Goal Pay Off Date:	Min Repayment:

DATE	REPAYMENT	BALANCE	NOTES

Expense *Tracker*

JAN ○ FEB ○ MAR ○ APR ○ MAY ○ JUN ○ JUL ○ AUG ○ SEP ○ OCT ○ NOV ○ DEC ○

DATE	DESCRIPTION	AMOUNT	NOTES

TOTAL ______________________

Credit Card *Tracker*

JAN ○ FEB ○ MAR ○ APR ○ MAY ○ JUN ○ JUL ○ AUG ○ SEP ○ OCT ○ NOV ○ DEC ○

DATE	CREDIT CARD	CREDIT LIMIT	%RATE	AMOUNT DUE	AMOUNT PAID	BALANCE

Monthly Financial *Reflection*

JAN ○ FEB ○ MAR ○ APR ○ MAY ○ JUN ○ JUL ○ AUG ○ SEP ○ OCT ○ NOV ○ DEC ○

TOTAL INCOME	TOTAL EXPENSES	DIFFERENCE	BALANCE

Biggest Wins this Month

What am I grateful for?

What do I need to improve for next month?

What did I learn by tracking my finances this month?

Wish *List*

JAN ○ FEB ○ MAR ○ APR ○ MAY ○ JUN ○ JUL ○ AUG ○ SEP ○ OCT ○ NOV ○ DEC ○

WISH LIST	HOPE TO PAY	WHERE TO BUY	BOUGHT	SPENT	SAVED	NOTES
			☐			
			☐			
			☐			
			☐			
			☐			
			☐			
			☐			
			☐			
			☐			
			☐			
			☐			
			☐			
			☐			
			☐			
			☐			
			☐			
			☐			
			☐			
			☐			
			☐			
			☐			
			☐			
			☐			
			☐			

Emergency Fund *Tracker*

JAN ○ FEB ○ MAR ○ APR ○ MAY ○ JUN ○ JUL ○ AUG ○ SEP ○ OCT ○ NOV ○ DEC ○

AMOUNT NEEDED:	TARGET DATE:
MONTHLY SAVINGS TARGET:	ACCOUNT:

Progress Tracker

10%	20%	30%	40%	50%	60%	70%	80%	90%	100%

DATE	DEPOSIT	WITHDRAW	NOTES	BALANCE

Notes

Credit Networking and *Mentorship*

JAN ○ FEB ○ MAR ○ APR ○ MAY ○ JUN ○ JUL ○ AUG ○ SEP ○ OCT ○ NOV ○ DEC ○

Networking Goals

What specific goals do you have for networking this month?

1 ______________________________

2 ______________________________

3 ______________________________

Mentorship Goals

What do you want to achieve with the help of a mentor this month?

1 ______________________________

2 ______________________________

3 ______________________________

Identify Networking Opportunities

Events & Workshops

List credit-related events, workshops, or webinars to attend this month:

1 ______________________________

2 ______________________________

3 ______________________________

Online Communities

Identify online groups or forums where you can engage with others focused on credit improvement:

1 ______________________________

2 ______________________________

3 ______________________________

Track Your Progress

Networking Activities

Record your networking activities for the month (e.g., events attended, new connections made):

1 ______________________________

2 ______________________________

3 ______________________________

Mentorship Activities:

Record your interactions with mentors (e.g., meetings, advice received):

1 ______________________________

2 ______________________________

3 ______________________________

Notes

____

____

____

Charity and *Giving*

JAN ○ FEB ○ MAR ○ APR ○ MAY ○ JUN ○ JUL ○ AUG ○ SEP ○ OCT ○ NOV ○ DEC ○

DONATION	ORGANIZATION	DATE GIVEN	VALUE	TAX DEDUCTIBLE

Self-care and Financial *Health*

JAN ○ FEB ○ MAR ○ APR ○ MAY ○ JUN ○ JUL ○ AUG ○ SEP ○ OCT ○ NOV ○ DEC ○

Self-Care Reflection

- **Physical Well-being**

  What physical health activities will you focus on this month?

  ○ ______________________________

  ○ ______________________________

- **Emotional & Mental Wellness**

  What mental health activities will you focus on this month?

  ○ ______________________________

  ○ ______________________________

- **Time for Self-Care**

  How will you make time for yourself?

  ○ ______________________________

  ○ ______________________________

Financial Health Reflection

- **Current Financial Practices**

  What financial habits do you want to maintain or improve this month?

  ○ ______________________________

  ○ ______________________________

- **Financial Goals**

  List your financial goals for this month

  o ______________________________

  o ______________________________

- **Financial Self-Care**

  How will you manage financial stress?

  o ______________________________

  o ______________________________

Accountability & Progress

- **Support System**

  Who will help you stay accountable this month?

  o ______________________________

  o ______________________________

- **Tracking Progress**

  How will you monitor your progress? (e.g., weekly check-ins, journaling)

  o ______________________________

  o ______________________________

- **End-of-Month Review Date**

  Set a date to review your goals and make any necessary adjustments

  o ______________________________

December

SMART Financial Goals *Worksheet*

JAN ○ FEB ○ MAR ○ APR ○ MAY ○ JUN ○ JUL ○ AUG ○ SEP ○ OCT ○ NOV ○ DEC ○

Description of Goals					
SPECIFIC Cost					
MEASURABLE Monthly Amount					
ATTAINABLE Method/Steps					
REALISTIC Goal Length					
TIMEBOUND Your Timeline					

Notes

Monthly Budget *Planner*

JAN ○ FEB ○ MAR ○ APR ○ MAY ○ JUN ○ JUL ○ AUG ○ SEP ○ OCT ○ NOV ○ DEC ○

INCOME	AMOUNT
TOTAL	

EXPENSES	AMOUNT
TOTAL	

BILLS	AMOUNT
TOTAL	

DEBT	AMOUNT
TOTAL	

SAVINGS	AMOUNT
TOTAL	

SUMMARY	AMOUNT
INCOME	
BILLS	
SAVINGS	
EXPENSES	
DEBT	
TOTAL	

Bills Payment *Calendar*

JAN ○ FEB ○ MAR ○ APR ○ MAY ○ JUN ○ JUL ○ AUG ○ SEP ○ OCT ○ NOV ○ DEC ○

SUN	MON	TUE	WED	THU	FRI	SAT
○ ○	○ ○	○ ○	○ ○	○ ○	○ ○	○ ○
○ ○	○ ○	○ ○	○ ○	○ ○	○ ○	○ ○
○ ○	○ ○	○ ○	○ ○	○ ○	○ ○	○ ○
○ ○	○ ○	○ ○	○ ○	○ ○	○ ○	○ ○
○ ○	○ ○	○ ○	○ ○	○ ○	○ ○	○ ○

Debt Repayment *Plan*

JAN ○ FEB ○ MAR ○ APR ○ MAY ○ JUN ○ JUL ○ AUG ○ SEP ○ OCT ○ NOV ○ DEC ○

Creditor:	Debt Type:
Starting Balance:	Credit Limit:
Repayment Frequency:	Interest Rate:
Goal Pay Off Date:	Min Repayment:

DATE	REPAYMENT	BALANCE	NOTES

Expense *Tracker*

JAN ○ FEB ○ MAR ○ APR ○ MAY ○ JUN ○ JUL ○ AUG ○ SEP ○ OCT ○ NOV ○ DEC ○

DATE	DESCRIPTION	AMOUNT	NOTES

TOTAL ____________________

Credit Card Tracker

JAN ○ FEB ○ MAR ○ APR ○ MAY ○ JUN ○ JUL ○ AUG ○ SEP ○ OCT ○ NOV ○ DEC ○

DATE	CREDIT CARD	CREDIT LIMIT	%RATE	AMOUNT DUE	AMOUNT PAID	BALANCE

Monthly Financial *Reflection*

JAN ○ FEB ○ MAR ○ APR ○ MAY ○ JUN ○ JUL ○ AUG ○ SEP ○ OCT ○ NOV ○ DEC ○

TOTAL INCOME	TOTAL EXPENSES	DIFFERENCE	BALANCE

Biggest Wins this Month

What am I grateful for?

What do I need to improve for next month?

What did I learn by tracking my finances this month?

Wish *List*

JAN ○ FEB ○ MAR ○ APR ○ MAY ○ JUN ○ JUL ○ AUG ○ SEP ○ OCT ○ NOV ○ DEC ○

WISH LIST	HOPE TO PAY	WHERE TO BUY	BOUGHT	SPENT	SAVED	NOTES
			☐			
			☐			
			☐			
			☐			
			☐			
			☐			
			☐			
			☐			
			☐			
			☐			
			☐			
			☐			
			☐			
			☐			
			☐			
			☐			
			☐			
			☐			
			☐			
			☐			
			☐			
			☐			
			☐			
			☐			

Emergency Fund *Tracker*

JAN	FEB	MAR	APR	MAY	JUN	JUL	AUG	SEP	OCT	NOV	DEC
○	○	○	○	○	○	○	○	○	○	○	○

AMOUNT NEEDED:	TARGET DATE:
MONTHLY SAVINGS TARGET:	ACCOUNT:

Progress Tracker

10%	20%	30%	40%	50%	60%	70%	80%	90%	100%

DATE	DEPOSIT	WITHDRAW	NOTES	BALANCE

Notes

Credit Networking and *Mentorship*

JAN ○ FEB ○ MAR ○ APR ○ MAY ○ JUN ○ JUL ○ AUG ○ SEP ○ OCT ○ NOV ○ DEC ○

Networking Goals

What specific goals do you have for networking this month?

1 ______________________________

2 ______________________________

3 ______________________________

Mentorship Goals

What do you want to achieve with the help of a mentor this month?

1 ______________________________

2 ______________________________

3 ______________________________

Identify Networking Opportunities

Events & Workshops

List credit-related events, workshops, or webinars to attend this month:

1 ______________________________

2 ______________________________

3 ______________________________

Online Communities

Identify online groups or forums where you can engage with others focused on credit improvement:

1 ________________________________

2 ________________________________

3 ________________________________

Track Your Progress

Networking Activities

Record your networking activities for the month (e.g., events attended, new connections made):

1 ________________________________

2 ________________________________

3 ________________________________

Mentorship Activities:

Record your interactions with mentors (e.g., meetings, advice received):

1 ________________________________

2 ________________________________

3 ________________________________

Notes

Charity and *Giving*

JAN ○ FEB ○ MAR ○ APR ○ MAY ○ JUN ○ JUL ○ AUG ○ SEP ○ OCT ○ NOV ○ DEC ○

DONATION	ORGANIZATION	DATE GIVEN	VALUE	TAX DEDUCTIBLE

Self-care and Financial *Health*

JAN ○ FEB ○ MAR ○ APR ○ MAY ○ JUN ○ JUL ○ AUG ○ SEP ○ OCT ○ NOV ○ DEC ○

Self-Care Reflection

- **Physical Well-being**

  What physical health activities will you focus on this month?

  - ______________________________
  - ______________________________

- **Emotional & Mental Wellness**

  What mental health activities will you focus on this month?

  - ______________________________
  - ______________________________

- **Time for Self-Care**

  How will you make time for yourself?

  - ______________________________
  - ______________________________

Financial Health Reflection

- **Current Financial Practices**

  What financial habits do you want to maintain or improve this month?

  - ______________________________
  - ______________________________

- **Financial Goals**

  List your financial goals for this month

  - ______________________________
  - ______________________________

- **Financial Self-Care**

  How will you manage financial stress?

  - ______________________________
  - ______________________________

Accountability & Progress

- **Support System**

  Who will help you stay accountable this month?

  - ______________________________
  - ______________________________

- **Tracking Progress**

  How will you monitor your progress? (e.g., weekly check-ins, journaling)

  - ______________________________
  - ______________________________

- **End-of-Month Review Date**

  Set a date to review your goals and make any necessary adjustments

  - ______________________________

Glossary of *Terms*

Annual Percentage Rate (APR): The interest rate charged on borrowed money, expressed as a yearly percentage. APR includes both the interest rate and any fees associated with the loan or credit.

Assets: Things that you own that have value, such as property, savings, investments, and personal belongings.

Bankruptcy: A legal process in which a person or business who can no longer pay their debts may seek relief from some or all of their debts through a court procedure.

Budget: A financial plan that outlines your income and expenses. It helps track your spending and ensures you live within your means.

Capital: The money or assets invested in a business or used for financial gain. In personal finance, it refers to the amount of money you have available for investing or saving.

Credit Bureau: A company that collects and maintains information about consumers' credit histories. The three major credit bureaus in the U.S. are Equifax, Experian, and TransUnion.

Credit Card: A payment card issued by financial institutions that allows you to borrow funds to make purchases, with the promise to pay back the amount, usually with interest, over time.

Credit Report: A detailed record of your credit history that includes your borrowing and repayment activity, such as credit cards, loans, and any late payments. It is used to assess your creditworthiness.

Credit Score: A number that reflects your creditworthiness, based on your credit history and financial behavior. Scores generally range from 300 to 850, with higher scores indicating better creditworthiness.

Credit Utilization Ratio: The percentage of your available credit that you're currently using. A lower ratio is considered favorable, as it indicates you're not overly reliant on credit.

Debt-to-Income Ratio (DTI): A percentage that compares your monthly debt payments to your gross monthly income. Lenders use this ratio to determine your ability to manage monthly payments.

Default: Failure to make required payments on a debt, such as a loan or credit card, according to the terms agreed upon.

FICO Score: A brand of credit score created by the Fair Isaac Corporation, used by lenders to assess a borrower's credit risk. It ranges from 300 to 850, with a higher score indicating better credit.

Fixed Interest Rate: An interest rate that remains constant throughout the life of a loan or credit agreement, making it predictable and easier to budget for repayments.

Inflation: The rate at which the general level of prices for goods and services is rising, and subsequently, purchasing power is falling. It can impact your savings and investment returns.

Interest: The cost of borrowing money, typically expressed as a percentage of the principal (the amount borrowed). It's paid to the lender in exchange for using their money.

Investment: The act of putting money into an asset or venture with the expectation of generating a return or profit, such as stocks, bonds, real estate, or mutual funds.

Late Fee: A charge imposed by a creditor or lender when a payment is made after its due date.

Liability: A financial obligation or debt, such as a loan or credit card balance, that you are legally required to pay back.

Loan: Money that is borrowed from a lender, such as a bank or financial institution, that must be repaid with interest over a specified period.

Minimum Payment: The smallest amount you can pay toward your credit card or loan balance without facing penalties. It usually covers the interest and a small portion of the principal.

Net Worth: The difference between your assets (what you own) and liabilities (what you owe). It represents your overall financial health.

Payment History: A record of your payments, including whether they were made on time or late. This is a significant factor in determining your credit score.

Principal: The original sum of money borrowed or invested, excluding interest. In a loan, it's the amount you borrowed, and in an investment, it's the initial amount you invested.

Refinance: The process of replacing an existing loan or mortgage with a new one, usually with better terms, such as a lower interest rate.

Secured Loan: A loan that is backed by collateral, such as a car or home, which the lender can claim if you default on the loan.

Unsecured Loan: A loan that is not backed by collateral. These loans are based on your creditworthiness and are riskier for lenders, which often leads to higher interest rates.

Student Loan: Money borrowed to pay for education-related expenses, such as tuition, books, and living costs. Student loans often have special repayment plans.

Tax Deductions: Expenses that can be subtracted from your taxable income to reduce your overall tax liability. Common deductions include mortgage interest, student loan interest, and charitable donations.

Tax Credit: An amount of money that can be subtracted directly from the taxes you owe, reducing your total tax bill.

Variable Interest Rate: An interest rate on a loan or credit that can change over time, usually based on market conditions or an index rate.

Wealth Building: The process of accumulating assets over time, through savings, investments, and other financial strategies, to increase one's financial security and net worth.

Withholding: The amount of money that is deducted from your paycheck for taxes, Social Security, and other federal or state obligations.

Zero-Based Budgeting: A budgeting method in which every dollar of income is allocated to specific expenses, savings, or debt repayment, leaving no income unassigned.